thefirstyears

thefirstyears

a parent & caregiver's guide to helping children learn

Foreword by Rob Reiner

LONDON, NEW YORK, DELHI, SYDNEY,
MUNICH, PARIS AND JOHANNESBURG

LONDON, NEW YORK, DELHI, SYDNEY,
MUNICH, PARIS, AND JOHANNESBURG

Book Designer: Megan Clayton
Project Editors: Nancy Burke and Jennifer Williams
Jacket Designer: Dirk Kaufman
Art Director: Tina Vaughan
Photography: Kellie Walsh
Publisher: LaVonne Carlson
Production Manager: Chris Avgherinos

First American Edition, 2001
00 01 02 03 04 05 10 9 8 7 6 5 4 3 2 1
Published in the United States by
DK Publishing, Inc.
95 Madison Avenue
New York, New York 10016

Dorling Kindersley Publishing, Inc. offers special discounts for bulk
purchases for sales promotions or premiums. Specific, large-quantity
needs can be met with special editions, including personalized
covers, excerpts of existing guides, and corporate imprints.
For more information, contact Special Markets Department,
Dorling Kindersley Publishing, Inc. 95 Madison Avenue,
New York, NY 10016 Fax: 800-600-9098.

Library of Congress Cataloging-in-Publication Data

Go, Joanne J.
       The first years : a parent and caregiver's guide to helping
children learn / Joanne J. Go, Janet R. Pozmantier, Laurie Segal
Robinson.--
1st American ed.
    p. cm.
    Includes index.
    ISBN 0-7894-8040-9
    1. Child rearing. 2. Child development.   I. Pozmantier, Janet R.
II. Robinson, Laurie Segal. III. Title.
    HQ774 .C36 2001
    649'.1--dc21

                            2001001478

Reproduced by Colourscan, Singapore
Printed in Italy by Lego

See our complete catalog at

www.dk.com

contents

getting to know me
birth to nine months

i can do it myself
9 - 18 months

on my way
18 - 36 months

foreword

Dear Parent: Raising a child is the most important job you'll ever have. No matter what your own experiences have been, you will naturally have a lot of questions and concerns when you come home with a new baby. How can you provide your child with the best nutrition? How often should you visit the doctor? What do you do when your baby won't stop crying? Will you ever get enough sleep again? I am the father of three young children myself, and my wife and I have seen firsthand how challenging it is to find the right answers to those questions – and all the others that are sure to arise. That's why I am so pleased to be able to join with DK Publishing to bring you the information and help that this wonderful book provides.

When I founded the *I Am Your Child* Foundation, I was motivated by research showing that secure and loving attachments with parents and caregivers, along with the right kind of developmental experiences, help give children the social, emotional, and cognitive abilities they need to reach their greatest potential in school – and in life. I wanted to let people know that babies and young children depend on rich interactions with adults (parents, grandparents, and others who care for them) to give them steady positive support and offer them stimulating experiences to help them grow and develop.

There are many things you can learn from this book that will help you create a positive, nurturing environment for your child. So relax a little, learn as much as you can, and most importantly, enjoy the wonderful adventure that you have just begun.

Rob Reiner
Founder, *I Am Your Child* Foundation

introduction

Becoming a parent is a life-changing experience, and the most important work you will ever perform. Knowing more about each stage of your baby's development makes it easier to understand and meet your baby's needs – an essential part of building a foundation of trust between you and your child. This trust, combined with a loving and nurturing environment, sets the stage for early learning, and encourages the development of confidence and self-esteem.

This book provides basic information about the first years of life. You will learn how your child develops from a tiny, vulnerable newborn to an active, independent toddler. You will gain an awareness of your infant's developmental needs, which will help you recognize your little one's "teachable moments." Most importantly, you will learn ways to build a strong – and lifelong – relationship with your child.

As a parent, you are your child's most influential teacher. This book is a guide to the most challenging part of parenting – helping your child develop social and emotional well-being. All parents want their children to grow into happy, healthy adults, and the first three years of life are vital to that growth. Learning about the importance of attachment and how to handle aggression are just two examples of the social and emotional issues highlighted in this book.

Although the term "parent" is used most frequently, this book is also addressed to all loving adults who interact with babies in the important first years of life. Caregivers of infants and toddlers will find much useful information here as they nurture the children in their care.

As you read this step-by-step guide to parenting, remember that all children are different. Following your loving instincts is just as important as the guidelines in this book. Above all, enjoy your baby!

We offer our best wishes as you embark on the greatest of life's journeys – parenthood.

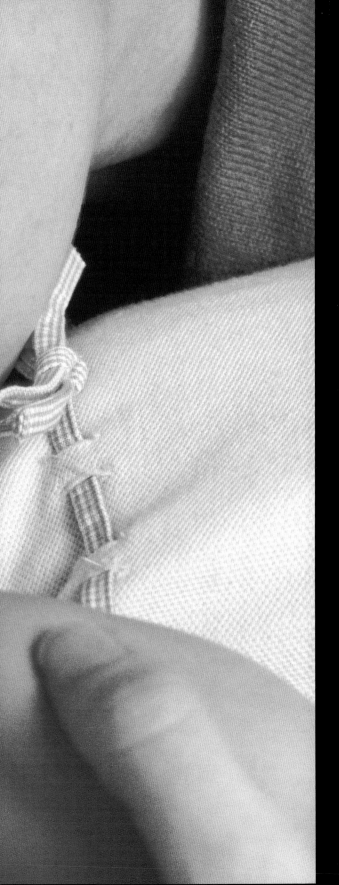

getting
toknow
me

birth - 9 months

— • —

Many new lessons await the parents of a newborn. As you strive to teach your baby about night and day, she teaches you how to comfort and hold her, and whether she likes to be rocked or held close and still. During this time you learn much from your relationship with this tiny bundle of joy.

— • —

developmental milestones

EVELOPMENTAL MILESTONES ARE THOSE IMPORTANT "FIRSTS" that show you how quickly your infant is growing. Almost every week you notice your baby is learning new skills. These are milestones that delight both you and your baby!

MILESTONE CONCERNS

It is natural to chart your baby's progress according to developmental milestones, but remember that each baby develops new skills at her own pace. However, if your baby seems delayed by more than two months in one or more of these developmental areas — for example, if your infant (three to six months old) does not turn her head when she hears your voice or does not follow movements with her eyes — the delay may indicate that she cannot see or hear as well as she should. If you notice other delays in language, social, or emotional development, mention your concerns to the pediatrician at your next well-baby visit. Many problems, if detected early, can be treated and successfully managed.

Although pediatricians advise parents not to put infants to sleep on their stomachs, you can place your baby on her tummy during playtime. She enjoys seeing the world from this new perspective — and it helps strengthen her arm and neck muscles.

birth to three months

Your newborn spends most of the time sleeping. She cannot do anything for herself. When awake, she looks at you, opens her eyes when held erect, and turns her head toward any source of steady sound. By the end of her second month, your infant cries energetically and begins to smile. She also kicks, coos, gurgles, and investigates parts of her body. She shuts her eyes when dazzled by bright light.

three to six months

Between three and six months of age, your baby begins to sit with support and bear her weight on her legs. She babbles, gurgles, laughs out loud, has a social smile, and anticipates food on sight. She also places her hands on the breast or bottle when feeding, looks at objects as small as a raisin, and looks for toys when they drop. Your baby begins to reach and grasp for objects, and when placed on her stomach, she can lift her head and shoulders.

six to nine months

By now your baby can sit alone, unsupport-ed, for an extended period (over one minute). Amazingly, she gets her feet to her mouth! When sitting, she reaches forward to grasp a toy with one hand without falling. She has learned to transfer toys from one hand to another. She may even attempt to crawl. Your baby now responds to her own name and imitates sounds that you make. She has come to expect the regular routines that you have established, and begins to enjoy peekaboo. She loves to play, persists in getting toys, and picks up a toy she drops. She bites and chews toys, and likes to make sounds with toys. She can also pronounce single consonants, such as: *ba, ka, ma*.

WHEN TO CALL THE PEDIATRICIAN

Your infant cannot tell you when she is in pain, but as you learn to read her cues, you will know how to comfort her (at least most of the time). However, if she cries inconsolably or develops a fever, call your doctor. During the first year, take your baby to her doctor at one month, two months, four months, six months, nine months, and twelve months. The American Academy of Pediatrics recommends your baby get shots to protect her against diseases such as polio, diphtheria, and hepatitis, starting with her two-month visit.

BIRTH THROUGH NINE MONTHS

touch**and**holding

AS A NEW PARENT YOU RECEIVE LOTS OF WELL-MEANING ADVICE. Sorting out the "do's" and "don'ts" of baby care can be a challenge, especially when some advice is based on long-standing traditions. For example, one old-fashioned belief is that going to a baby every time she cries "spoils" her. New research shows quite the opposite. Far from spoiling a child, loving touch and frequent holding help babies form secure attachments and help to build a foundation for healthy emotional development and a happy life.

the importance of "attachment"

NURTURING AND AFFECTIONATE PHYSICAL contact – kissing, stroking, massaging, holding, and cuddling – form the basis of attachment. ATTACHMENT is the special love relationship that forms between a newborn infant and her parent.

A child who forms a secure attachment to at least one parent learns faster, feels better about herself, and makes friends more easily. Cuddling and nurturing also help your baby handle stress and, over time, can support her capacity to regulate her own emotions. According to some experts, early feelings of competence help children become more capable and confident as adults. When you think about it, it feels right to hold and kiss your baby. So go ahead and do it – you can't love your baby too much!

Research shows that touching and holding your infant stimulates her brain to grow and make connections that are vital to her emotional health.

can a baby "control" an adult?

A POPULAR MYTH ABOUT BABY care is that picking up your infant whenever she cries teaches her how to control you – and to cry more often so that she controls you even more. This is not possible because infants under one year of age have not developed the skills necessary to "control" an adult. On the contrary, when you respond to your baby's cries, she learns that you can be counted on to help her with all her needs. She learns to trust you. As she gets older, this trust provides security, and she is more likely to develop the ability to communicate with you in other ways – such as talking – and even to wait for you without crying, knowing you always come.

Loving touch, gentle hugs, and lots of kisses and cuddles strengthen the unique, loving bond between your baby and you.

HOW TO HANDLE WELL-MEANING "ADVICE"

Figuring out your new role as parent is hard enough, so the avalanche of well-meaning advice from friends and relatives that often arrives with the baby can make things even more confusing! How can you respond to a beloved friend or close relative whose advice doesn't feel right to you? Be kind, yet firm. You can say that you appreciate the advice and will give it some serious thought, but continue to do what you think is best for your baby. After all, you are the parent!

13

feeding**issues**

EEDING IS THE MOST BASIC OPPORTUNITY FOR YOU AND YOUR NEW BABY to connect with each other; it is also crucial to your infant's health. During the first weeks you may find it challenging to feed your newborn, whether you decide to breast-feed, bottle-feed, or both. Be patient and remember that your baby is just beginning to learn about how things work in his world.

babies and feeding schedules

FEED YOUR NEWBORN WHENEVER HE is hungry. Trying too hard to get your new baby on a feeding schedule can do more harm than good. He may get overly hungry between feedings, then get frustrated and stop feeding because he cannot get enough milk at one time. Feeding your baby when he is hungry meets both his nutritional and emotional needs. Not only does he get his tummy filled, he also learns to trust those around him to take care of him in other ways. Over time, you begin to recognize when your baby is "telling you" he is hungry. Perhaps he cries in a certain way, or sucks on his thumb after waking from a nap. Eventually, he and you establish a schedule.

INFORMATION ABOUT BREAST-FEEDING

Although breast milk is the healthiest choice for feeding your infant, breast-feeding does not come naturally. Both you and your baby have to learn how to do it. You can get help with breast-feeding through the hospital or birthing center where you delivered, or through La Leche League, an international organization that is dedicated to helping women with lactation support and information. Many communities have other lactation consultants as well. Take special care to drink plenty of fluids and eat a balanced diet, which increases your milk supply if you are breast-feeding, and it helps keep you healthy.

advantages of breast-feeding

BREAST-FEEDING, BY ITS VERY nature, is an especially satisfying way to connect with your infant. Breast milk is also the best nutrition for your growing baby, because it strengthens his immune system, giving him more resistance to bacteria and disease. Even if you breast-feed for only a couple of weeks, your infant becomes better protected against germs and illnesses than a baby who only drinks formula. This is because you pass your body's immunities to your baby through your breast milk. However, there are some circumstances when breast-feeding should be avoided. If you are HIV-positive, have AIDS, or have a problem with alcohol or drugs, do not breast-feed. Be sure to ask your doctor any other questions you may have about breast-feeding.

getting close during feeding

YOU CAN ALSO MAKE A POWERFUL connection with your newborn through bottle-feeding. In fact, this is an excellent way for dads and other family members to form a loving and lasting bond with the little guy. Hold the baby close to you, cuddle him, look into his eyes, and talk or sing to him while giving him the bottle. These soothing rituals make the feeding experience enjoyable for both of you!

FEEDING TIPS

❖ Feed your baby on demand, even if he wants to eat every hour. Eventually his feedings become more spaced out.

❖ Do not worry about whether your baby is getting enough milk, especially if you are breast-feeding. If your baby seems to be full and content after feedings, wets 6 to 8 diapers in a 24-hour period, and is gaining weight, everything is going just fine.

❖ Try to stay relaxed. When you are tired or stressed, your milk supply can decrease.

❖ If you continue to breast-feed after returning to work, you can express (or pump) and refrigerate your milk before you leave home or during work.

❖ If your baby was born pre-maturely, or is very sensitive to stimuli, slow down and focus on one activity at a time. For example, don't rock your baby while you are feeding him.

❖ At about four months old, your baby may find it difficult to settle down at feeding times, or to start and finish his milk all at once. This happens because your baby becomes more aware of his world and interested in all the new, exciting things around him.

sleepissues

EFORE THERE WAS A BABY IN YOUR LIFE, you probably took sleep for granted. Even if you were aware that new parents don't sleep much, you had no way to "save up sleep" beforehand to help you sail through the newborn period. Now that you are sleep-deprived, you may worry that you will never feel completely rested again. Relax! Your baby will sleep, and you can help him do it.

   In the meantime, remember to take good care of yourself. Try to sleep when your baby sleeps. The cooking and cleaning may not be up to the usual standards, but your health — physical and mental — is more important. If you sleep whenever you can, you feel better, which benefits both you and your baby.

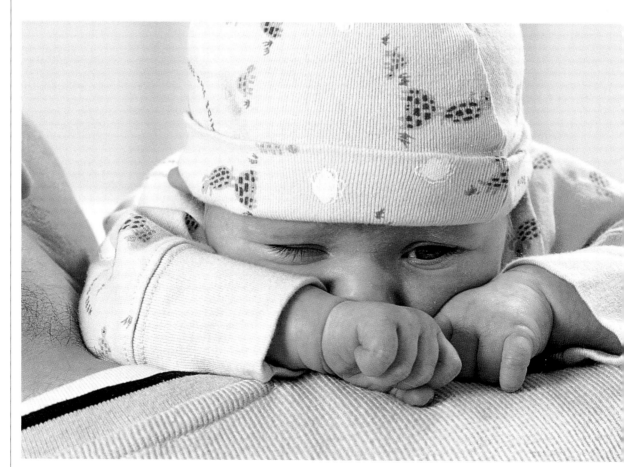

All children are different, of course, but most newborns sleep 4 or 5 hours at a time before waking to be fed. As they get older, infants *sleep longer between feedings. By the end of the first year, most babies sleep 7 to 12 consecutive hours at night.*

Special bedtime routines, such as cuddling and singing lullabies, help infants relax and settle down for the night.

helping your baby sleep

YOUR BABY FALLS ASLEEP MORE EASILY IF YOU FOLLOW the same routine at the same time every night. Routines help babies learn predictable patterns, and if the same routine is followed every night – for example – a bath followed by feeding and bed, your baby soon understands what to expect. Just knowing what comes next helps him approach bedtime more calmly. Many babies and their parents also love sitting together in a rocking chair before bedtime. During this special time of closeness, you can read or sing to your baby. As soon as he gets drowsy, settle him into his bed. If you wait until he is asleep, however, he may become dependent on you to rock him to sleep. And try to put him to bed early enough so the adults in the family can get some rest, too!

IF YOUR BABY CRIES AT BEDTIME

If your baby cries when you put him to bed, he needs to be assured that he is not being abandoned. Here are some suggestions to help your baby settle down for the night:

❖ Sit or stand just outside of your baby's sight, and whenever he pauses between cries, tell him in a very quiet voice that you are there.

❖ Do not pick up your baby (unless he is crying from pain) or turn on the light; these actions keep him from getting sleepy.

These suggestions should help your baby learn to feel secure in the knowledge that when he is in bed, you are still there for him. He may cry for an hour the first night (which can be pretty hard on parents!), but every night gets better. Within a few weeks, he should cry very little or not at all when you put him to bed.

establishing**routines**

WHEN YOUR BABY ENTERS THE WORLD, first encounters and new experiences can sometimes be disturbing. Diaper changes, baths, and other "firsts" are often met with tears from your little bundle of joy. And for good reason. Infants express fear by crying, and your baby's first reaction to anything new may well be fear. But when an experience is repeated over and over, your baby becomes familiar with it and a pattern – or "template" – is formed in her mind. The repeated experience becomes a predictable routine that your baby comes to expect and even welcome.

the positive effects of establishing routines

WHEN CARING FOR YOUR BABY, REMEMBER THAT DOING things the same way each time – and even doing daily activities in the same order – helps her feel safe and secure. When your child is a toddler, and bedtime becomes more of a challenge, an evening routine can work as a tool to help her wind down after a busy day. A little farther down the road, self-control comes more easily when a predictable schedule is in place. When children know what the rules are and what to expect, they respond more positively to your requests. Routines are a great way to establish order and a sense of security for both parents and children.

HOW YOUR INFANT'S PERSONALITY GROWS: BUILDING TRUST

Renowned psychoanalyst and teacher Erik Erikson believed that an individual's personality develops in eight stages over a lifetime. More importantly, each stage contains a basic task that must be successfully completed so that healthy development can progress to the next stage. Stage one occurs during the first year of a child's life – when she begins the task of learning to trust. You can help your infant accomplish this task by remembering that . . .

❖ During the first stage of personality development, your baby is totally dependent on you to meet all her needs.

❖ How you respond to your infant's needs, and how you display affection, directly influence her ability to feel safe, and therefore develop trust.

❖ You can help your baby develop trust by paying close attention to the signals she sends you about her needs and preferences, and by responding to them warmly and predictably.

Make bathtime a regular part of your baby's evening routine. Bathing is great fun for your infant and you, and the warm water helps her calm down for sleep.

howbabiescommunicate

INFANTS COMMUNICATE FROM THE MOMENT THEY ARE BORN. The hour following birth is a quiet-alert state when the newborn makes direct eye contact with her mother and father as they hold her and look into her eyes. This is an important step in getting to know one another. If your baby was born prematurely, had special needs that were attended to immediately after birth, or was adopted, you may have missed this experience. Rest assured that you have many opportunities to bond later.

YOUR NEWBORN'S BEHAVIORAL STATES

❖ **Quiet sleep**: breathing is smooth and rhythmic; eyelids are closed with no eye movement; body is relaxed.

❖ **Active sleep**: breathing alternates between rapid and slow; eyelids are closed with rapid eye movement (REM); body may twitch and baby may cry.

❖ **Drowsy**: state between sleeping and waking; eyelids open and close; body moves more.

❖ **Quiet-alert**: eyes are open; baby makes eye contact and cooing sounds; body is inactive. Newborns are in the quiet-alert state about 10% of the time; this is the best state for playing and interacting with your infant.

❖ **Active-alert**: body moves in rhythmic cycles; baby may become overstimulated and look away when tired.

❖ **Fussy, crying**: body moves vigorously; skin may be flushed.

reading your baby's cues

AT FIRST IT MAY SEEM AS IF THE ONLY way your baby can communicate with you is through crying. Beyond the distinctive cries – from fussing, to whimpering, to all-out wailing – your newborn gives you many other cues. Her changing behavioral states (see sidebar) are another way of "telling" you what she likes and dislikes, wants, or needs. For example, in the quiet-alert state your newborn is most receptive to some type of play or interaction. She clearly signals her readiness by quieting her body, making direct eye contact with you, and cooing.

On the other hand, a simple yawn may not be so simple at all. Your baby may be signaling that she is tired. Or she may be "saying" that she is overstimulated and needs a break.

Eventually you are able to "read" all your infant's cues. Her eye contact, smiles, gurgles, whimpers, fussiness, cooing, or babbling "tell" you when she is happy, hungry, uncomfortable, needs a diaper change, wants to play, or just enjoys being cuddled.

THE FAMILIARITY OF YOUR VOICE

Child development expert and pediatrician, T. Berry Brazelton, uses a technique to show a new parent something special: Just a few days after birth a baby shows a strong preference for a parent's voice. Dr. Brazelton holds the newborn in his arms, directly between himself and the parent. Then he and a parent both speak to the baby using the same volume and tone of voice. They actively compete for the infant's attention. The baby may turn her head this way and that at first, but within a few moments she turns her head completely towards her parent. Already she responds to the voice that is most familiar to her!

When your baby is three or four months old, she enjoys "talking" playfully with you. Say something to her, wait for a response, then imitate whatever sounds she makes. Continue this back-and-forth "conversation," and you are soon happily cooing at each other.

talking "parentese"

PARENTS INSTINCTIVELY USE A KIND OF speech, called PARENTESE, when talking to their baby. They speak in a high-pitched tone because newborns and young babies are naturally more responsive to high-pitched voices and sounds, such as "baby talk." Although you may have heard that parents should not use "baby talk" with children, speaking this way to your infant is perfectly fine. Your newborn cannot, in fact, understand the actual words you use. But she does understand the emotions behind them, and she listens carefully to the rhythm of your voice. When you sing, babble, or use "baby talk," notice how your baby's eyes light up as she looks into your face. She may even reach out to touch your neck or mouth. You are teaching her the sounds and rhythms of language, as well as the patterns of communication.

Holding your baby is another way to communicate with her. During these times of quiet cuddling and playing, you may even feel that she is talking back to you with her eyes.

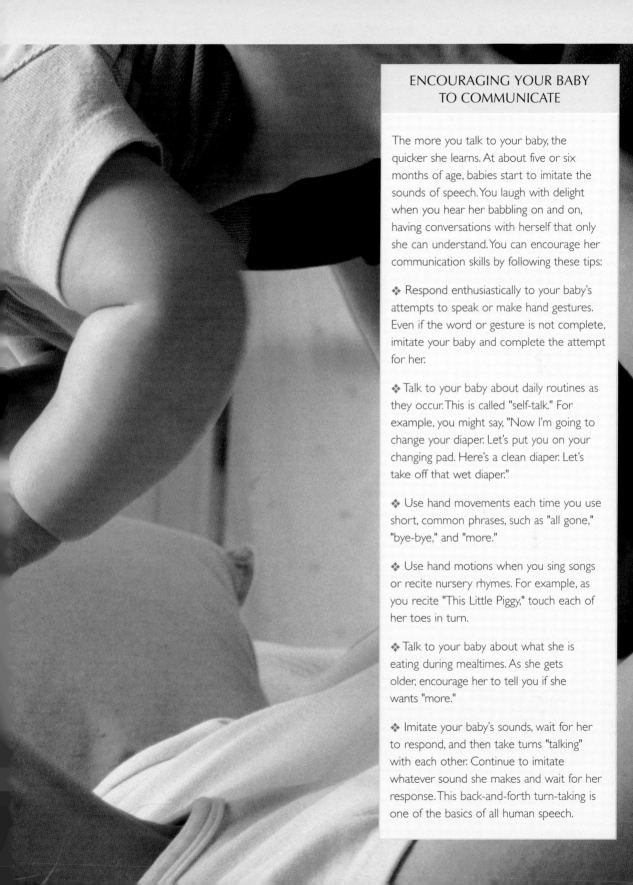

ENCOURAGING YOUR BABY TO COMMUNICATE

The more you talk to your baby, the quicker she learns. At about five or six months of age, babies start to imitate the sounds of speech. You laugh with delight when you hear her babbling on and on, having conversations with herself that only she can understand. You can encourage her communication skills by following these tips:

❖ Respond enthusiastically to your baby's attempts to speak or make hand gestures. Even if the word or gesture is not complete, imitate your baby and complete the attempt for her.

❖ Talk to your baby about daily routines as they occur. This is called "self-talk." For example, you might say, "Now I'm going to change your diaper. Let's put you on your changing pad. Here's a clean diaper. Let's take off that wet diaper."

❖ Use hand movements each time you use short, common phrases, such as "all gone," "bye-bye," and "more."

❖ Use hand motions when you sing songs or recite nursery rhymes. For example, as you recite "This Little Piggy," touch each of her toes in turn.

❖ Talk to your baby about what she is eating during mealtimes. As she gets older, encourage her to tell you if she wants "more."

❖ Imitate your baby's sounds, wait for her to respond, and then take turns "talking" with each other. Continue to imitate whatever sound she makes and wait for her response. This back-and-forth turn-taking is one of the basics of all human speech.

crying

WHEN YOU SEE PARENTS AND THEIR BABIES in magazines or on television commercials, they are happy and smiling. The reality, of course, is that babies are not always happy and smiling – and neither are their parents. Babies cry! Why they cry, how much crying is considered normal, and what to do about crying are questions all new parents need answered.

GROWING CONFIDENT CHILDREN

Nearly 30 years ago, child development researchers discovered that infants whose parents are responsive to them cry less and communicate their needs better (without crying) in the second year of life. They are more confident and self-reliant as one- and two-year-olds. This shows that when you respond to your baby's cries with hugs and soothing words he learns that you care for him. This "early learning" provides a firm basis for self esteem.

why babies cry

WHEN YOUR BABY CRIES, HE IS communicating his feelings, or needs. He is trying to let you know that he may be lonely, hungry, tired, cold, frustrated, sick, frightened, or just plain uncomfortable. Simply put, your infant cries because he needs your help. And crying is the only means he has – right now – to ask for that.

You may be able tell the difference between your newborn's cries after just a few weeks. For example, a whining cry may mean that your baby is hungry. A fussy cry may mean that he needs to be burped, have a diaper changed, or is simply uncomfortable. Older infants may fuss when they are teething. If your baby whimpers, especially in his crib, he may be trying to comfort himself and get back to sleep – or he may have lost his pacifier.

If your baby is wailing – a high-pitched, uncontrollable cry – he could be very uncomfortable or hungry. If the crying continues despite your efforts to calm him, he may be in pain, and you should call the pediatrician right away.

colic versus normal crying

MOST NEWBORNS CRY FOR A COUPLE of hours every day. This is normal. But some newborns cry much more, for a variety of reasons, including anything from anxious parents to milk allergies to colic. COLIC refers to prolonged periods of crying or screaming that can last from one to four hours. Episodes usually occur in the late afternoon or early evening, for no apparent reason. A newborn who suffers from colic may clench his fists, draw his legs up to his chest or stomach, and cry so hard his face turns red. Although colic has no cure or treatment, it also has no harmful effects. However, episodes of colic can be very frustrating for parents because they typically occur at the time of day when parents are the most tired.

Ask your pediatrician to give you specific suggestions about colic. For example, your doctor may recommend changes in your diet if you are nursing. The good news is that colic usually goes away by the time your baby is three to five months old.

Many parents find their baby's crying the most difficult part of caring for him. Remember that crying is the only way he can communicate with you. He is trying to let you know that he needs you.

Responding to your baby's cries with warm hugs and comforting words teaches him that he is loved and that he can trust you to take care of his needs. This is the most important thing you can do to encourage his healthy emotional development.

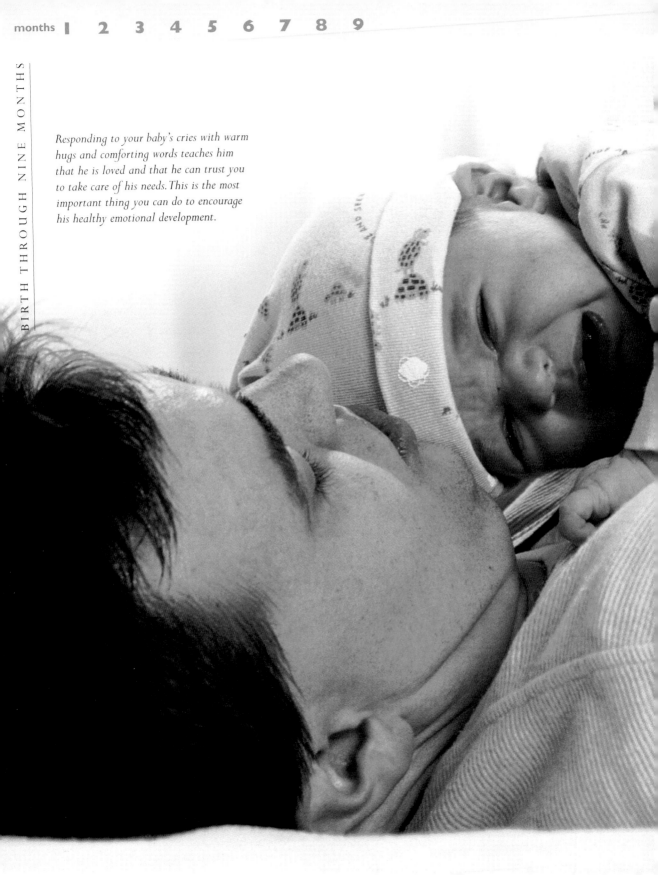

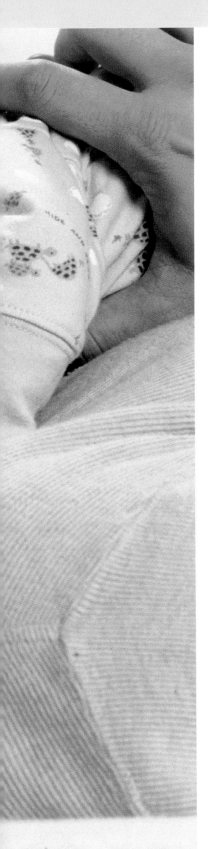

what to do when your baby cries

THERE ARE MANY POSSIBLE responses to crying, depending on your cultural background. The following responses are some basic suggestions that offer a good place to start.

Go to your baby as soon as you can. Just being there helps him learn to trust that you will take care of him.

Hold your baby. He enjoys hearing the rhythmic beating of your heart and may calm down when you hold him close.

Relax. Your baby may be reassured by your quiet mood and stop crying.

Take a walk. Put your baby in his stroller or an infant sling and go for a long, relaxing walk.

Sing! Your baby loves to hear you sing, whether you know all the words to every nursery rhyme or even sing on key.

Babies also love the soothing motion of a rocking chair, or the soft "jiggling" motion you can make while your baby rests on your legs or in your arms. But remember: Never shake your baby!

When your baby cries, try massaging him. He may be calmed by the soft, rhythmic touch of your fingers.

Put your baby in his car seat and take a drive. The motion of the car and the vibration of the engine can have a soothing effect.

Even vacuuming the house can distract and soothe a crying baby. Settle him comfortably in a secure place and start cleaning the carpets!

Put your baby in his infant swing and gently start to move him. The back and forth motion often has a tranquilizing effect.

Remember, different things work for different babies. So you may have to try several of these suggestions to find what works best for your baby.

HELP FOR THE CRY-WEARY PARENT

If your baby cries a lot, you may feel overwhelmed or even angry at times. This is natural – many new parents feel this way. The around-the-clock demands of a newborn are exhausting. When you add sleep-deprivation and a daily routine that has been thrown completely out of whack, is it any wonder you feel overwhelmed? If you start to feel this way, put your baby safely in his crib and take some "time out" for yourself. Better yet, ask someone to fill in for you for a while, so you can take time to calm down, get out of the house for an hour or two – or get some sleep!

temperament

WHEN YOUR BABY IS BORN, you may expect her to be just like you, but do not be surprised if she turns out to be quite different! Even from birth, you can notice an infant's unique temperament traits. TEMPERAMENT is the set of characteristics that describes how your child deals with the world around her. Is your baby easy or difficult to comfort? Is she slow and cautious, or active and impulsive? Unpredictable, or routine-oriented? These are just some of the temperament traits you may recognize in your infant.

NINE TEMPERAMENT TRAITS

This guideline is useful in determining your infant's unique temperament.

❖ **Activity level**: Is she relaxed and calm or always ready to go?

❖ **Distractibility**: Is she easily distracted or can she concentrate when there are activities and noise around her?

❖ **Persistence**: Does she stick with tasks or give up easily?

❖ **Approach**: Does she approach new things quickly or is she slow to warm up?

❖ **Intensity**: Are her emotional reactions mild or dramatic?

❖ **Adaptability**: Does she adapt easily to change or resist change?

❖ **Regularity**: Does she respond well to routines or is she unpredictable?

❖ **Sensory threshold**: Is she sensitive to physical stimulation or is she mellow?

❖ **Mood**: Is she carefree or serious?

responding to your infant's unique temperament

RECOGNIZING YOUR CHILD'S temperament traits is essential to understanding why she behaves in certain ways. It also helps you choose the most effective parenting style for her. In fact, a good match between her personality and the way you respond to it may solve, or even prevent, some behavior "problems." For example, some children are very sensitive to the feel of certain fabrics. Your baby may cry, seem uncomfortable, or even resist you when you try to put certain clothes on her. Instead of assuming that you have a "difficult" child or getting angry while dressing her, simply eliminate the clothes that cause her distress.

Remember that although you cannot change your child's temperament, you can help her adjust to the world around her by the way you react.

"GOOD" VERSUS "BAD" TEMPERAMENT TRAITS

There are no "good" or "bad" temperament traits, although some children have a more challenging mixture of traits. On the other hand, it can be just as much of a challenge when the parents' temperament traits are quite different from their child's.

Be aware that parents and children who have different temperament styles can learn and benefit from each other. If you are very structured, for example, and your child is not, you may learn from her how to "let go" and have fun. In return, your child may learn from you how to be better organized (and even clean her own room someday!).

play

PLAYING WITH YOUR NEWBORN COMES NATURALLY. Just pay attention to her changing behavioral states, or moods. They provide important clues about how much interaction your baby wants. For example, the best time to play with your infant is during the "quiet-alert" state (see sidebar on page 20). You may notice that as your baby tires, her eye contact with you decreases, or she may fuss or cry because she is overstimulated. Respond to her cues by allowing her to rest for a while.

Hold up a mirror so that your baby can see herself. While she does not yet know that she is seeing her reflection, her happy and surprised reactions let you know that she is enjoying herself.

The best time to playfully interact with your newborn is during the "quiet-alert" state, when her eyes are open and making contact with yours, and her body is still. Sometimes she makes cooing sounds in response to your playful mood.

playing with your newborn

TAKE PLENTY OF TIME TO FEED, diaper, and dress your newborn. If you are not rushed, you may use these opportunities to have fun with your baby. No special toys are required, just you. Try wiggling parts of your body, or your baby's body, play peekaboo with clothing, or make funny noises. Simply talk to her.

You may feel a little silly at first, but watch her responses. She enjoys seeing your mouth move and hearing the sounds you make. She lets you know she is having fun by beginning to smile, coo, and make noises when you speak to her.

Another fun activity is trying to get your baby to look at and grasp a rattle. Hold the rattle about ten inches away from your baby's face and shake it to get her attention. If she reaches out for it, place the rattle in her hand, hold it there, and shake it gently to teach her

> ## WHEN PLAYTIME IS OVER
>
> If you see your newborn losing interest in play, first try changing activities. Watch your infant's face to see which activity she likes best. If she continues to turn her head away, she may be letting you know that she needs a rest. Playtime is over for now.

how to do the same. After a few times your baby learns to do this by herself.

playing with your older baby

WHEN YOUR BABY IS ABOUT SIX MONTHS OLD, she tries to copy what you do when you play games, such as peekaboo. She learns so many things from this type of game. For example, it prepares her for copying you when she learns new tasks, such as eating by herself, learning to talk, and even putting on clothes.

As your baby begins to roll and crawl, join her on the floor and see what the world looks like from her perspective. The floor is one of the best places to play with your child, now and for years to come. When you are down at her level, she can take the lead in the games you play.

Your baby does not need fancy toys to have fun. All she really needs is you — her first and best playmate. In fact, she enjoys just looking at you.

SIMPLE HOMEMADE TOYS

Some of the most fun toys for babies can be made simply and easily at home. Here are a few ideas:

❖ Make a simple mobile to hang above your baby's changing table or crib. Use contrasting black and white triangles or bright colors. Leave the pieces blank or draw funny faces on them for your baby to look at.

Remember that she will be looking at the mobile while lying on her back, so make sure the mobile pieces hang down horizontally, facing her.

❖ Stuff a knee-high stocking with a handful of crisp cellophane (tie it off or sew it at the top) to make a soft, crinkly toy for your baby to touch and hold.

❖ Make a sock puppet and wear it on your hand to entertain your infant. If you choose a white sock, use a permanent marker to draw on eyes, nose, and mouth. If you use a colored sock, sew on felt pieces in a contrasting color for the eyes, nose, ears, and mouth. Use your creativity to make an animal's face!

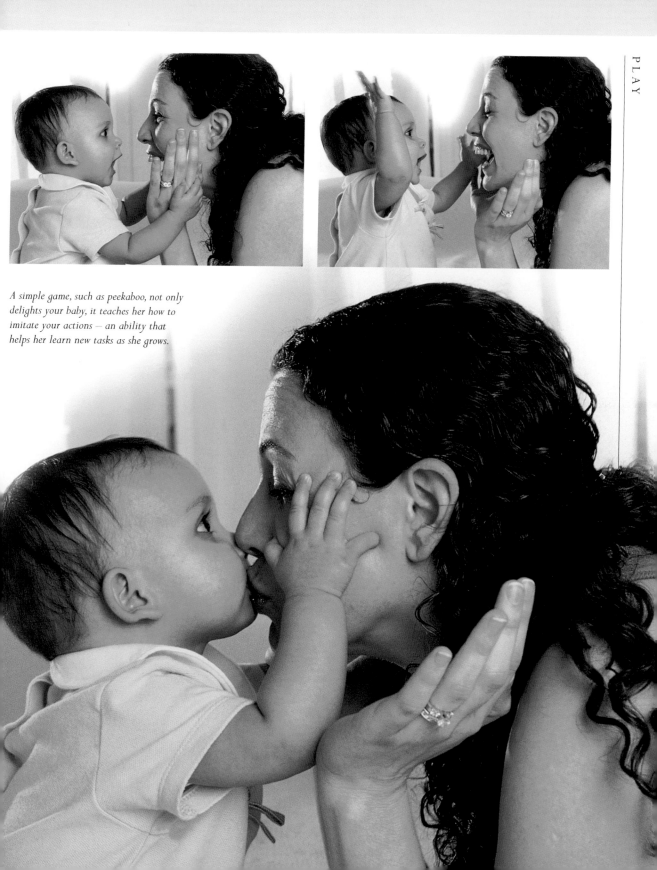

A simple game, such as peekaboo, not only delights your baby, it teaches her how to imitate your actions — an ability that helps her learn new tasks as she grows.

how babies learn

IMPORTANT LEARNING TAKES PLACE from the earliest weeks and months of an infant's life. In fact, scientists have found that the early years are a time of active brain development, and that the kinds of experiences and attachments young children have can be especially important to that development. Consistent nurturing develops a strong emotional attachment between you and your infant, as well as positive, healthy feelings in your baby. The closer the bond between your baby and you, the more eager he is to learn everything!

the importance of touch

GENTLY TOUCHING AND CUDDLING your baby makes him feel safe and secure. In fact, some experts believe that loving touch helps stimulate and "grow" your baby's brain, so that when he gets older he is more capable of loving other people. So snuggle up with your baby as often as you can, but do not overstimulate him. Be gentle and responsive to the cues he gives you. If he likes what you are doing – great! But if he frowns or pulls away, be aware that it is time to stop.

learning through repetition

BY SIX TO EIGHT WEEKS OF AGE, YOUR infant has already developed expectations from repeated interactions with the important adults in his life. For instance, when you hold your baby upright in your arms, he knows this is a position for interaction. He naturally becomes more alert – and either "expects" something to happen or initiates an interaction himself. For example, a bouncy, quizzical look at Dad might indicate his readiness for play, while an "all business" glance at Mom may signal his desire to be fed.

As early as two months old, your infant looks forward to your nurturing care.

learning through frustration

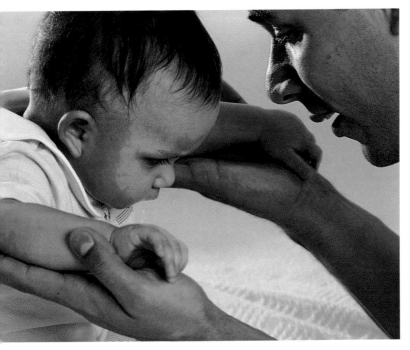

As your baby becomes more mobile, he hurries to get upright – first sitting, then creeping or scooting along. Even at a few months of age, your infant strains to get himself up when you gently pull his arms. He may get frustrated when he tries to move in a certain way that is difficult for him – but that's okay! These frustrations are all part of the learning process. If you rush to help him too often, he does not experience the success of doing something all by himself.

With a little help and encouragement from you, your baby tries to pull himself up to a standing position. Remember to be gentle with your baby's arms when you help him get up.

MOUTHING, LOOKING, AND TOUCHING

Your baby learns important lessons about his world by simply looking, mouthing, and touching almost everything. Be on the alert for these infant learning milestones:

❖ **Mouthing**: Your baby works hard to put things in his mouth. This is the primary way he explores and learns. Allow him to mouth objects that are clean and safe – and large enough that he cannot choke on them. If your baby wants to chew on books, do not worry. Choose a few soft cloth or plastic books that can take the wear and tear – and moisture – of a curious little one.

❖ **Looking**: As early as two months of age, your little one watches a mobile for extended periods of time and even tries to stay awake to do so. He also watches his hands, turning them over and over in front of his eyes. He is beginning to learn hand-eye coordination. This "practice" helps him when he starts reaching out to touch objects, at about four months of age.

❖ **Touching**: Infants really start to use their hands at about three months of age. Giving your baby rattles, plastic cups, and safe, simple toys helps him build strength and coordination. At about four months, he starts learning how to transfer toys from one hand to the other. He also touches your face: This is the beginning of what is called **PERSON PERMANENCE**, the awareness that people are real and continue to exist even when out of sight. As he learns to move about more, at around seven months, your infant tests this new concept by hunting for toys, pushing them out of reach, and then going after them again.

Mouthing and touching objects also help your baby develop an understanding of dimensions – for example, depth and distance – which in turn helps his visual perceptions become clearer.

redirection
and childproofing

TEN TIPS FOR CHILDPROOFING

❖ Hide electrical cords and cover electrical outlets with special plastic guards.

❖ Keep your baby's crib away from window coverings or cords.

❖ Pick up any small objects such as paper clips, thumbtacks, coins, and gum that may have fallen on the floor. Your baby could choke on them.

❖ Lock cabinets that contain poisonous substances, such as cleaning products, or relocate them to an over-the-counter cabinet.

❖ Keep medicines and foods that your baby can choke on, such as nuts, hard candy, and popcorn, out of reach.

❖ When cooking, always turn pot handles toward the stove.

❖ Pad sharp corners on furniture so that your baby does not hurt herself.

❖ Relocate plants to higher ground.

❖ Make a special cabinet for your baby's toys so that she can reach them easily.

WHEN A CRAWLER IS EXPLORING HER WORLD, your job is to make sure that world is a safe place to navigate. To get a better understanding of what your baby encounters at her eye level, get down on your hands and knees and look for anything that could be harmful to her, then remove it. No matter how well you childproof your home, accidents can still happen. That is why you should always supervise small children — and practice steering them away from anything that can harm them.

the meaning of redirection

IMAGINE THAT YOUR EIGHT-MONTH-old has crawled over to the corner of the living room and has just noticed an uncovered electrical outlet. Just as she is ready to investigate, you turn around and see what is about to happen. You have several choices: You can yell at your child, spank her hand, or redirect her. All three options can stop your baby, but only one has a long-lasting, positive outcome — redirection.

REDIRECTION means changing direction. If your baby starts to head toward a harmful activity or object, the best solution is to remove it or steer her away from it, and distract her with one of her own toys or another safe activity.

WHAT TO DO WITH YOUR VALUABLES

Your baby eventually learns to respect objects — but not at this age. First of all, young infants and toddlers are not capable of understanding the concept of "respect." Second, breakable objects need to be treated gently, but small children do not yet have the ability to control their physical strength. If you leave delicate things on a coffee table, you may spend lots of time either correcting your child or getting angry over broken valuables. Neither response creates a positive interaction with your baby. Put breakable objects away or up on a high shelf for now. Later, when your child is much older, you can bring them down and teach her to handle them gently.

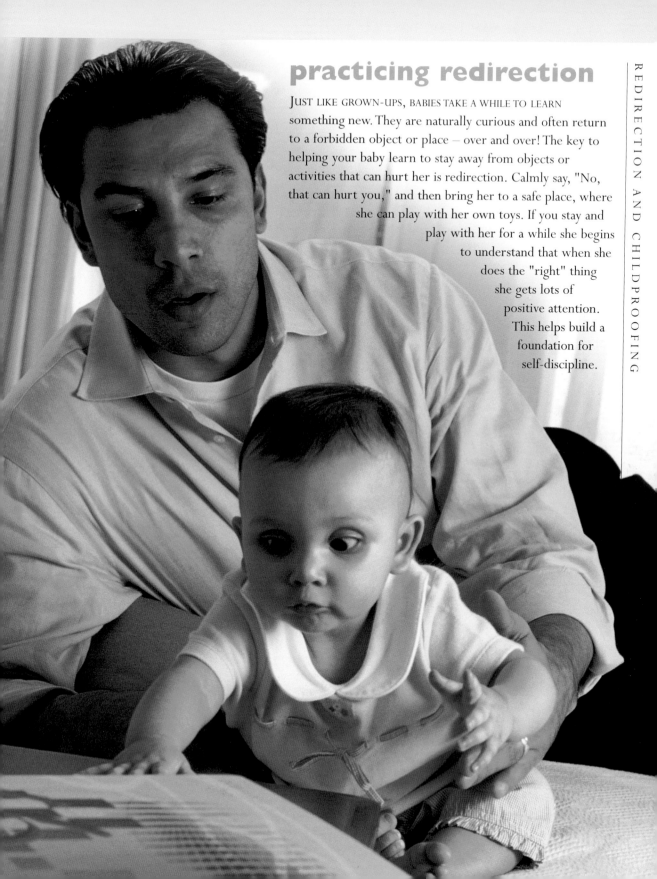

practicing redirection

JUST LIKE GROWN-UPS, BABIES TAKE A WHILE TO LEARN something new. They are naturally curious and often return to a forbidden object or place – over and over! The key to helping your baby learn to stay away from objects or activities that can hurt her is redirection. Calmly say, "No, that can hurt you," and then bring her to a safe place, where she can play with her own toys. If you stay and play with her for a while she begins to understand that when she does the "right" thing she gets lots of positive attention. This helps build a foundation for self-discipline.

stranger**awareness**

BABIES ARE MUCH MORE AWARE OF THEIR WORLD – even at birth – than many of us realize. For example, a new baby knows her mother's voice and scent and can identify her from other adults. Throughout the newborn period, an infant continues to develop her senses, learn more about her world, and distinguish between familiar and unfamiliar people, places and objects. As your baby's senses develop more fully, so does her ability to think, leading her to become "wary" of strangers.

understanding stranger awareness

FEARFUL RESPONSES TO STRANGERS may happen when your baby tries to figure out so much about a person that she is overwhelmed. At about five months of age, your baby may get upset if someone she does not know well approaches her too closely or makes direct eye contact with her. If that person then tries to pick her up, she may become more upset and cry, because now that person has intruded into her personal space.

This wariness of strangers is called STRANGER AWARENESS. It begins at birth and gradually increases, peaking at about eight months of age, and ending around your baby's first birthday. Of course, each child is unique and goes through this stage with different degrees of intensity and for longer or shorter periods of time.

anger at an "absent" parent

IF WORK TAKES YOU AWAY FROM home on a regular basis, you may meet with a cool reception from your child when you return. In fact, she may act like she has never met you before. Worse, she may cry and reject you when she first sees you.

Remember that your absence has required her to make a big adjustment, just when she is starting to understand that you still exist even when you are out of sight. If your baby cries after you have been away, she may be "saying" she is angry at you for going away. You may even seem disturbingly unfamiliar to her, depending on how long you have been gone.

To ease the situation, always say good-bye each time you leave your child. If you have to travel for a few days, be sure that her other parent or caretaker mentions you often – perhaps counting down the days until you return. Have a photograph taken of your baby and you that she can keep at child-care so that she can always "see" you.

HELPING YOUR BABY "SAY" GOOD-BYE

This period in your baby's life can make saying good-bye difficult. You can do several things to help ease the loud protests you are likely to hear when the time comes to leave your infant:

❖ Make sure you leave your baby with someone who understands the situation – preferably someone with whom your baby is very familiar.

❖ Let your baby know when you are leaving and when you are coming back. You might say, "Mommy's going to go bye-bye now. I will see you this afternoon, after playtime."

❖ Have a special blanket or toy ready, especially in a child-care setting. Your baby may find it comforting to have a familiar object with her.

❖ Keep to a routine as much as possible during this stage.

Predictability is comforting to children, especially during difficult times. At home, keep morning and evening routines the same. At child-care, before you say good-bye, play a familiar game with your baby or sing a favorite song each time you leave. When you pick up your child at the end of the day, give her a special hug or greeting.

Children who are in a child-care setting often save up their emotions for the end of the day when they are back at home with the people who make them feel safest. Your little one may even begin to cry as soon as you appear, but try not to take it personally. She is just letting go of pent-up emotions. When you finally get home, spend some quiet time cuddling with your baby or perhaps rocking her. In a short while, she feels reconnected and back on track.

i can do it myself

9 - 18 months

———— • ————

An awareness of your
child's specific developmental
needs helps you recognize
his "teachable moments."
As he toddles toward
independence, you provide
him with a safe environment
for the exploration and
play that are so important
for his growth.

———— • ————

9 THROUGH 18 MONTHS

developmental milestones

D EVELOPMENTAL MILESTONES ARE THOSE IMPORTANT "FIRSTS" that let you know how quickly your older baby is growing. You are constantly amazed at how fast your 9- to 18-month-old child changes and learns new skills. Here we highlight some of the skills you can look for.

9 to 12 months

Your baby can pull to a sitting position and sit steadily for more than ten minutes. She learns to crawl, begins to walk, and uses her fingers to feed herself. She can also drink from a cup using two hands, and she lifts her arms for her shirt to be put on. She likes to play and cooperates in games. She tries to roll a ball to another person and offers a toy without releasing it. Sometimes she even amuses herself for short intervals. She shows interest in pictures and uncovers toys. She begins to put things in and out of containers and to drop objects deliberately. She reaches with her index finger and waves good-bye. She follows some simple commands with gestures, such as "Come here," and under-stands "No" – or its inflection. She says "Mama" or "Dada" – randomly at first, then meaningfully. By 12 months of age, she can say at least one other word.

WHEN TO CALL THE PEDIATRICIAN

Your baby is learning to communicate and may sometimes be able to tell you when she is in pain (though not very clearly). She may pull at her ears or say her tummy hurts. Ask your baby to show you where it hurts. She may not know the word for "throat," but if she points to her neck she probably has a sore throat. If her complaints are accompanied by fever, or continue over a period of time, call your pediatrician. Schedule your child's well-baby checkups at 9 and 12 months of age. The 12-month pediatrician visit is a thorough checkup. Arrange a first visit to the dentist too, so your child avoids any serious dental problems.

Let your baby help with dressing and undressing, and encourage her efforts. It's a lot harder for her to put her socks back on again! Learning to get dressed by herself gives her positive feelings of indedpendence, too.

12 to 18 months

Your baby learns to stand alone, crawl up steps and onto furniture, and begins to walk unassisted. She cooperates in dressing by holding out her arms or legs, and taking off her socks. She eats with a spoon – with some spills – and she holds her own bottle or cup. She now points or makes a noise to indicate she wants something. She cries when she loses a toy and brings an object from another room when you ask for it. She is learning new words and imitates sounds. In fact, she "jabbers" in her own language, which seems to make sense to her. She imitates household activities. She scribbles spontaneously with a pencil or crayon, looks at pictures in a book, and stacks objects.

MILESTONE CONCERNS

Use these developmental milestones as a guideline to gauge how your child is growing and acquiring new skills. If you think your baby has a developmental delay or a disability, schedule a check-up with your pediatrician. If your doctor believes your baby needs extra help, he or she may refer you to an Early Childhood Intervention (ECI) program in your area. These programs evaluate and assist children who may have developmental delays or disabilities. They also assist the family and provide needed services at no cost. Do not hesitate to ask your pediatrician about other resources in your area. (For more information about how to seek Early Childhood Intervention, see the Resources section at the end of this book.)

from**crawling**to**walking**

THERE IS NOTHING QUITE LIKE THE FIRST TIME YOUR BABY MOVES — on his own — without your help. While you are thrilled that he has reached another important milestone, you may also feel a tinge of sadness because your baby will never be totally dependent on you again. Your positive reaction to his emerging independence helps him build confidence and self-esteem.

encouraging independence

YOUR CHILD DELIGHTS IN HEARING your encouraging words as he crawls, scoots, pulls up to stand, and then, takes those important first steps. Cheering him on with words – such as "Look at you, you can stand up! You can do it!" – makes him work even harder to master these new tasks. As you praise your baby's mobility, you also encourage him to enjoy his newfound independence. The pride he experiences in knowing you support his efforts enables him to feel good about himself and to develop a confident "I-can-do-it!" attitude towards trying new experiences.

Be sure to shower him with hugs and kisses when he is both successful and unsuccessful in his attempts: It is important that he keeps on trying, despite the setbacks that inevitably occur.

LEARNING TO WALK
— • —

Between six and ten months of age, your baby develops enough muscle strength and control to move around on his own. During this stage of development, it is important to encourage him to move freely, so be sure to limit his time in the playpen, stroller, and crib. He needs to be able to continue strengthening his muscles and to discover the many ways he can physically explore his world.

❖ **Sitting**: Your baby first learns to sit, then get up on "all fours" (on his hands and knees), and then rock back and forth in a crawling position.

❖ **Crawling**: When your child is comfortable with being on all fours,

he soon starts to crawl forward, using his hands and knees. Most babies crawl in this fashion. Some babies, however, scoot along on their bottoms, slide on their bellies, or even crawl backwards. Other babies never crawl at all, and go from sitting to pulling up and standing.

❖ **Pulling up and standing**: Your baby learns to stand by grabbing onto things and pulling himself up. He probably uses almost anything and everything to pull himself into a standing position, from coffee tables and bookshelves to the hem of Mom's skirt. At first, he is delighted to just stand and stand. In fact, babies who put lots of effort into learning

this new skill may even wake up during the night and pull up on the side of the crib to stand. At this point, your baby may "forget" how to sit back down, and cry for help. If this happens, go to him and gently help him sit down.

❖ **Walking**: Sometime between 8 and 18 months, your baby starts walking. In the beginning he does lots of "walking around" while holding on to furniture and other supports. Don't try to hurry him. When he feels ready, he begins experimenting with walking completely on his own – cautiously at first, then with greater and greater confidence.

Until he is walking regularly on his own, bare feet are best for learning to walk steadily.

SAFETY CONCERNS

❖ When your baby starts crawling, he still uses his mouth to help explore new objects. Childproof all electrical outlets, and be sure that the floor is free of any items that might be a choking hazard or that could injure him. (A great way for you to see things on his level is to get down on the floor and crawl around yourself.)

❖ When your baby first starts standing and then walking, remember that he is sure to have many stumbles and falls. Be sure to pad any sharp corners on tables and chairs to prevent cuts and bruises. Because he is "taller" now, he also explores higher terrain – reaching for, grabbing at, and pulling down objects above him. He does not know his own strength yet, so if he grabs or pulls too hard, he may sometimes break things. Remove any breakable or dangerous objects within his reach. In the kitchen, childproof cabinet doors and turn pot handles toward the back of the stove.

❖ With greater mobility, your child needs more careful supervision. He quickly masters walking and then begins to run. Supervision at this stage means providing an environment that is safe, so that he can explore freely. Make sure you are always in the same room to oversee his activities.

ONE STEP AT A TIME

If you are the parent or caregiver of a baby who was born prematurely, he may start crawling and walking a little later than his full-term peers. Rest assured, he will eventually catch up. Your baby learns to move at his own pace and in his own way. Many babies, in fact, concentrate on learning to talk before they walk. However, if your child has not begun to crawl, scoot, stand, or walk by the time he is 12 months old, consult your pediatrician.

9 THROUGH 18 MONTHS

feeding

Y OUR OLDER BABY IS NOW SITTING IN A HIGH CHAIR FOR MEALS. While she still eats spoon-fed food, this is the age when she really enjoys using her hands to feed herself. She picks up and eats finger foods, such as cereal, soft vegetables, and fruit (peeled and cut into small pieces). Do not bother with plates or other table settings – simply spread finger foods right on the high chair feeding tray or tabletop. Be sure to serve her small portions, about one-fourth the amount an adult would eat, and be prepared for a big mess! Your baby does not yet have the ability to eat neatly.

encouraging your baby to use a spoon

WHEN YOUR BABY IS ABOUT 12 MONTHS OLD, HE MAY surprise you one day by grabbing the spoon from you and trying to feed himself. Let him. His attempts are awkward at first, and he has trouble getting the spoon into his mouth. With practice and encouragement, however, he eventually succeeds in feeding himself. Resist the temptation to continue spoon-feeding him (even though it would be a lot easier for you), as learning to feed himself is important to him. Gaining a sense of mastery ("I can do it!") is important to him developing his self-image and self-esteem. Your job is to tolerate his messes the best you can and serve as both teacher ("Hold it like this") and cheerleader ("You can feed yourself!").

learning to drink from a cup

YOUR PEDIATRICIAN MAY RECOMMEND THAT YOU SWITCH your baby from the breast or bottle to a cup when he is about one year old. A cup with a top and a spout is best, but it takes time and practice for your child to figure out how to drink from the cup without spilling the contents all over himself. Here is a helpful hint: Bathtime provides a fun way to help your baby practice this new skill. Just put him in the tub with a cup of juice. If he spills, he can easily be washed off.

FOODS TO "HANDLE WITH CARE"

Meat should be cut into small pieces and moistened with broth or gravy. Serve only soft, peeled fruit. Cut grapes in half and remove the seeds. Mash other fruit or cut it into small pieces. When your baby has a few teeth, he enjoys gumming hard foods such as frozen bagels.

Do not give honey or peanut butter to your child until he is at least one year old, as young children can be especially allergic to these foods.

To avoid choking, don't give your child hot dogs, gum, hard candy, popcorn, or nuts until he is at least five years old.

making sure your baby gets enough to eat

WHEN YOUR BABY STARTS FEEDING himself, you may be concerned that he is not getting enough to eat. In fact, most of his food may seem to end up on the floor, rather than in his mouth. Relax. Older babies go through a period when they eat less than they did during the first year of life, since they are not growing as rapidly. If you provide your baby with a variety of foods — from all of the food groups — and allow him to decide which foods and how much of each he wants to eat, he should be fine. Researchers point out that over the course of a week, most children naturally select all the nutrients they need from each of the food groups.

Remember that providing your baby with nutritious foods and encouraging good eating habits are gifts that last a lifetime.

AVOID FOOD BATTLES

Do not force your child to "clean her plate" or eat certain foods. Most experts agree it is best not to make an issue of uneaten food. These battles can make food an emotionally charged part of life. However, if your baby is losing weight, or seems to be ill, consult your pediatrician.

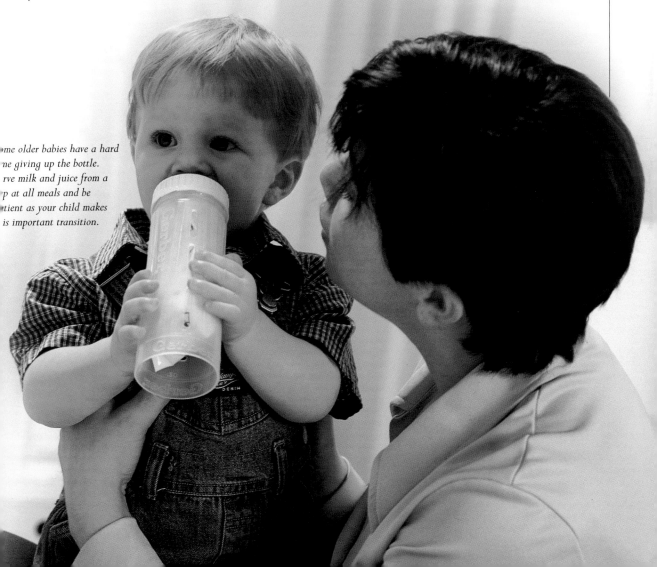

Some older babies have a hard time giving up the bottle. Serve milk and juice from a cup at all meals and be patient as your child makes this important transition.

9 THROUGH 18 MONTHS

settinglimits andgivingdirections

A S YOUR CHILD BEGINS CRAWLING AND WALKING, setting limits and giving clear directions helps keep her safe. Setting limits is a three-step process: establishing rules or boundaries about safety or behavior; teaching your child what those rules or boundaries are; and helping her to remember and follow them by giving her clear directions. Setting limits can involve a variety of issues – from serious safety concerns, such as not going into the street, to how loudly pots can be banged or how many cookies can be eaten. When you set limits, you help your toddler learn how to keep herself safe, and you also teach her how to become self-disciplined and considerate of others.

BREAKING RULES AND PHYSICAL PUNISHMENT

If your toddler breaks a serious rule – such as one about street safety – think twice about how you react. Spanking or slapping your child may stop her, but neither action is likely to teach her about safety. She may be so shocked and frightened by your behavior that instead of learning about street safety, your toddler learns that big people can hurt smaller and weaker ones. She may also learn that the people who love her can also hurt her. This kind of message weakens her trust in you and the loving bond you have worked so hard to build.

setting limits, teaching rules

THE BEST WAY TO SET LIMITS AND teach your child rules is to follow the SSPP formula: Say it, Show it, Practice it, and Praise it. For example, if you want your child to stay out of the street, follow these four steps:

Say "We walk to the sidewalk only, and no farther."

Show her the sidewalk and the street.

Practice walking with her to the sidewalk, then let her walk to the sidewalk by herself.

Praise her when she stops at the sidewalk – and give her a hug or kiss.

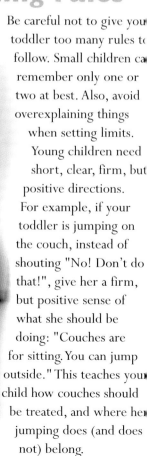

Be careful not to give your toddler too many rules to follow. Small children can remember only one or two at best. Also, avoid overexplaining things when setting limits. Young children need short, clear, firm, but positive directions. For example, if your toddler is jumping on the couch, instead of shouting "No! Don't do that!", give her a firm, but positive sense of what she should be doing: "Couches are for sitting. You can jump outside." This teaches your child how couches should be treated, and where her jumping does (and does not) belong.

setting boundaries for appropriate behavior

SETTING LIMITS IS ALSO ABOUT establishing boundaries for appropriate behavior. If your child is banging the kitchen pots very loudly, for instance, try using the SSPP formula, follow these steps:

Say "All that noise hurts my ears. Please bang softly." This helps your toddler learn that people do not always like loud noises and begins teaching her about consideration.

Show her how to bang softly — she may not know how.

Practice banging softly with her, then let her try it on her own.

Praise her by saying, "You learned how to bang softly! What a smart girl." This strengthens her desire to

Everyday household items — are safe "toys" for your toddler. You may have to set limits if the noise gets too loud!

please you and helps her remember how to bang softly next time.

Practice and praise are key to setting limits successfully. Children remember the right way to do something when they do it several times — and when they are praised for doing it well.

USING THE "NO" WORD EFFECTIVELY

Save your "No's" for only the most serious situations. If your child hears the word "No" said too often on too many occasions, she may not pay attention when a "No" is really needed – for example, when she is about to do something dangerous. For most situations, tell your child what to do instead of saying "No." For example, if she starts pulling on a page in a book, try saying "Hold the page like this," and then show her how to do it.

learning

YOUR BABY IS MOVING INTO TODDLERHOOD — literally! First she crawls, then walks, then moves away from you to explore the world. She is learning how to separate from you, reconnect, and communicate with you. Your child now shows a preference for familiar people and looks to you for reassurance and encouragement. She loves learning new things — and she does not need expensive toys. All she needs is you, her first and best teacher, and a safe environment where she can explore all she wants.

learning through reading

NOW IS A GOOD TIME TO TEACH YOUR child that books are special. Create a library just for her, and keep her books on a low shelf that she can reach. (Place treasured books that you do not want torn on a higher shelf.) When creating her library, remember that toddlers love to look at books with pictures of young children doing a variety of things. If you are not sure what other books are right for your child, go to your local bookstore or library and ask for help. When you visit your library, find out if they have a "story hour" — kids love them!

Follow her lead as you look at books together. She may want to spend lots of time looking at some pictures, or she may turn the pages very fast.

how toddlers learn

PLAY IS YOUR CHILD'S MOST VALUABLE teaching tool. While she plays, she learns about how things work and about cause and effect. She learns best at her own pace and when she is self-directed. She also learns how to make things happen (and not happen) for herself. Pay special attention to the things that interest her most, then let your "teaching" take off from there, in a relaxed, natural way. If your child loves to play with cars and blocks, for example, she may build a road by placing blocks end to end. Simply watch her, at first, then help her extend her road with more blocks. When she tires of the game, stack the blocks on top of each other. She may knock them down to build another road – or she may imitate you and try to stack the blocks herself. Let her take the lead when she plays. (For more information about learning through play, see pages 54–56.)

language learning

ACQUIRING LANGUAGE IS A BIG PART of your child's learning experience. You already know how smart she is, but you have real proof that her mind is "working" when she starts to speak. How your child learns to speak is a complex process that develops over years. You can help her by remembering not to do all the talking and by following her cues. Listen to the sounds or words she makes, imitate what she is saying, and then wait for her response – just as if you were having a two-way conversation. (For other tips on how to encourage language learning, see "How babies communicate," pages 20–23.)

OTHER WAYS YOUR TODDLER LEARNS

Your young child learns a variety of valuable lessons by experimenting – through play – with these three powerful developmental concepts.

❖ **Imitation:** Your nine-month-old child can imitate everything, from funny faces to new noises. When you sing to her or recite nursery rhymes, she tries to mimic you. Her ability to imitate allows her to learn to be more and more like you, which makes her happy.

❖ **Causality:** Your young toddler is just learning how things work: why a toy moves or makes a noise; what happens when she drops something (Will Dad pick it up?). Soon she learns specifically how to make something happen, such as pushing a button on a toy to create a noise.

❖ **Storage:** Before the age of one, your baby is easily distracted. If you hand her a toy while she is holding another one, she drops the toy she is holding. When she is about a year old, however, she learns how to hold one toy in one hand and take a new toy in the other hand. If you offer her a third interesting toy, she may put one toy under her arm or in her mouth, so she has a free hand to grab the new object.

LEARNING AND THE PREMATURE INFANT

If your child was born prematurely, she may learn at a different pace than other children. Do not be concerned if it takes her longer than another child to learn the same task. Eventually she will catch up and learn everything she needs to. She just may have to work a bit harder at it than other children. What is important is that she continues to move forward at her own pace.

biting

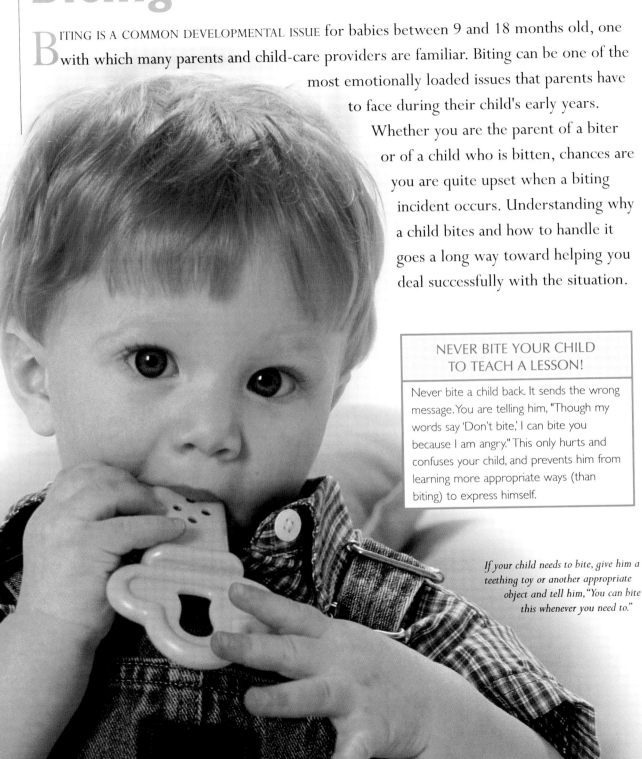

Biting is a common developmental issue for babies between 9 and 18 months old, one with which many parents and child-care providers are familiar. Biting can be one of the most emotionally loaded issues that parents have to face during their child's early years. Whether you are the parent of a biter or of a child who is bitten, chances are you are quite upset when a biting incident occurs. Understanding why a child bites and how to handle it goes a long way toward helping you deal successfully with the situation.

NEVER BITE YOUR CHILD TO TEACH A LESSON!

Never bite a child back. It sends the wrong message. You are telling him, "Though my words say 'Don't bite,' I can bite you because I am angry." This only hurts and confuses your child, and prevents him from learning more appropriate ways (than biting) to express himself.

If your child needs to bite, give him a teething toy or another appropriate object and tell him, "You can bite this whenever you need to."

why children bite

CHILDREN BITE FOR A WIDE RANGE OF reasons, from the very simple (being angry) to the more complex (being overstimulated). Child development experts have shown that almost all biting behaviors are related to physical, emotional, or social developmental issues.

Between the ages of about 5 months and 15 months, your child explores his world primarily by using his mouth. Sometimes that exploration turns into a bite.

If your child is teething, biting down on something eases the pain and helps him feel better. Sometimes a very young child cannot discriminate between safe objects to bite and people.

Your child may bite to communicate his needs and feelings, since he does not yet have the words to express what he wants. A bite may simply mean, "Leave me alone!" Child development experts call this type of biting PURPOSEFUL BITING.

Your older baby is now experimenting with the powerful concept of "cause and effect."

He quickly learns that when he bites he gets a big reaction.

Any significant changes in your baby's life – from a new sibling to a new home, from friction between parents to being placed in child-care – can make him anxious. Biting may be his way of expressing anxiety.

If your baby starts biting, he may be showing that he is frustrated. Most toddlers cannot communicate effectively, which can be very frustrating. He may express this feeling by biting.

Remember to be careful about how you handle your own feelings of frustration and anger. Do you lose your temper easily and scream when you are angry? Or do you verbalize your feelings?

Children first learn how to interact with their environment by watching you. They are keenly aware of how you respond to different situations, and they will mimic your behavior. If you get angry or lose control when you are frustrated, the likelihood that your child will respond in the same way is that much greater.

BITING IN THE CHILD-CARE SETTING

Since biting is a common developmental issue among young children, most child-care providers have experience in dealing with biting incidents. However, if your child bites or is bitten at child-care, do not hesitate to talk with his teacher and find out how the situation is being handled. A word of warning, though: If your child is bitten, do not expect to be told who the biter is. Child-care providers may not share this information.

HOW TO HANDLE BITING INCIDENTS

❖ Respond immediately to the situation.

❖ Separate the biter and the child who was bitten, and keep them separate for a while.

❖ Comfort the child who was bitten and make sure he is not seriously hurt. Check for broken skin, bleeding, or bruising, and take appropriate first aid measures.

❖ Do not overreact. Stay calm, but let the biter know that you do not approve of his behavior and that biting is not acceptable. Give him a stern look and say, "No biting people. It hurts!" Try to give the biter as little attention as possible. Attention can reinforce negative behavior.

❖ Explain to the biter how he can express himself in more acceptable ways. For example, you might tell him, "It's okay to feel mad, but it's not okay to bite people. Just say, 'I'm mad!' when you feel mad."

❖ If your child is teething, provide teething toys and crackers for him, explaining that he can bite these things, but not people.

❖ Reward good behavior. When your toddler resists biting and "uses his words" instead, be sure to praise him for what he has learned.

play

NOW THAT YOUR OLDER BABY IS MORE MOBILE AND INDEPENDENT, you can discover even more ways to play together – from physical play to word play to experimenting with new (and old) objects and activities. Watching your baby respond, learn, and gain control of a new toy or activity can be as exciting for you as it is for him.

HOW TO PLAY WITH YOUR OLDER BABY

Watch your child closely when he tackles a new activity, but also allow him the freedom to explore that activity by himself. Observe how he experiments with an old toy (such as a rattle) in different ways, and let his play take off from there. Wait to see what he does on his own with a new toy, before you show him the "magic button" that makes it work. You may notice that as he masters a new task, he is eager to move on to more challenging activities. Encourage him to do so. On the other hand, if a new activity or toy seems to be too difficult and frustrating for him, gently redirect him to a more familiar activity, and reintroduce the new toy or activity at a later time.

Paying attention to your child's general mood and behavior throughout the day can also help you determine the most appropriate play for him. A fussy toddler, for example, might enjoy close, quiet time – looking at a book, singing, or talking.

As your baby's attention span increases, he moves from thinking that something is only there when he sees it, to knowing that things still exist even when he cannot see them.

word play

YOUR BABY ENJOYS HEARING YOU RECITE SILLY RHYMES and nonsense words and add new and funny verses to familiar songs. At the same time he is also learning new things about sounds and language. In fact, the more you talk, sing, and have fun while you're playing with words, the more excited your baby becomes about learning. Simple games such as peekaboo and pat-a-cake also teach your child a great deal. Peekaboo in particular is great fun for your older baby because he is learning that people and objects are still there even when he cannot see them.

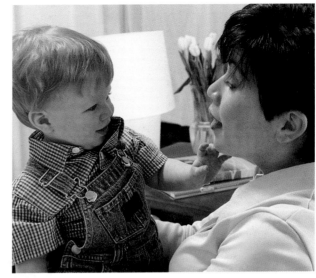

The more you talk, sing, and have fun while you play, the more excited your baby becomes about learning.

Fingerplay is also an important way for your child to learn. Beloved finger games such as "Tortillitas" and "Where is Thumbkin?" have been passed down from family to family for so many years that we do not know who played them first. They are favorites of children everywhere because of their gentle repetition. As you repeat the words or actions with your baby, he learns them too, and they soon become gifts you share with each other at playtime.

CREATING A SPECIAL PLACE FOR TOYS

One good idea is to have a low shelf in each room, for toys and other safe objects, that your child can reach by himself. Remember, you probably have many household objects that are more fun for your child to play with than expensive toys. Pots, pans, wooden spoons, and plastic dishes – placed on a low kitchen shelf – can keep your baby entertained while you are busy making dinner.

9 THROUGH 18 MONTHS

physical play

PHYSICAL PLAY IS SO MUCH FUN. You and your older baby enjoy rubbing noses with each other, tickling and giggling together, and even roughhousing on the floor. Remember, however, that very young children can often become overstimulated. Your baby is just learning how to regulate her young body, and her nervous system is still delicate. Too much tickling can actually be painful. Pay attention to any cues she gives you, however subtle, that she has "had enough." Teach her that it is okay to say, "Stop."

When you have had enough play, let your child know that with a firm, direct statement. For example, your child loves dropping objects and having you pick them up for her — over and over. Not only is this "game" great fun for her, it also reinforces her early learning about how objects disappear and reappear. When you are tired of picking up her spoon or toy from the floor, let her know that the game is over by saying, "That's enough now." If she does it again (and she will), repeat the same phrase and place the object out of her reach. She learns from this experience, too, just as she does from her playful interactions with you.

One of the fun things about parenting is being the one to introduce new activities to your baby. Watching your toddler respond, learn, and gain control of an activity can be as exciting for you as it is for her.

separation**anxiety**

DURING THIS STAGE OF YOUR BABY'S DEVELOPMENT, she may start to have a difficult time saying good-bye to you. Do not be surprised if she starts clinging to you and crying inconsolably whenever you try to leave her. She may even have trouble being in a different room. Your little one is most likely experiencing SEPARATION ANXIETY, a normal stage in a child's development that begins at about 9 months and peaks between 18 and 24 months.

why separation hurts

SEPARATION ANXIETY OCCURS because your baby cannot consistently form a mental picture of you that she can "carry" with her when you are not around. Her ability to do this continues to develop over the next few years – and throughout her life. For now, however, when you leave your toddler, she believes that you are gone forever! Allow your baby to go through this stage at her own pace. Separation anxiety eventually passes.

Providing your child with lots of love, security, and reassurance is the best medicine for separation anxiety.

other signs of separation anxiety

SEPARATION ANXIETY often goes hand in hand with other changes in your child's behavior or temperament that do not seem to be related to "separation" at all. For example, you may notice that besides having difficulty saying good-bye, your baby also has frequent tantrums when undergoing changes at home or at child-care. Or she may become quieter and start keeping to herself more. You may worry that something else is going on with her – and of course you should always check with your pediatrician or child-care provider to rule out other reasons for her behavior. Once you know that separation anxiety is the issue, however, you can do a number of things to help your baby through this stage.

MAKING SEPARATIONS EASIER

Your child's temperament and experiences with routine good-byes both play a role in how she handles separating from you. For example, if your child is more adaptable to new situations, she may find it easier to settle in and feel comfortable when you leave her. If she is resistant to change, your child may have more difficulty saying good-bye. Here are some ways to make separating easier.

❖ Never ridicule your child or tell her she is being "a baby." Separation anxiety is a very real fear.

❖ Try to keep your own stress levels down. When you are tense, your baby can sense it and separations become even more difficult.

❖ When you leave, make your good-byes as brief as possible. The longer the good-bye, the worse the separation experience for your child. Your young toddler benefits most from a quick good-bye ritual, such as a hug and kiss – and you telling her when you will be back.

❖ Whenever possible, keep changes in your child's daily routine to a minimum. Predictable routines increase your child's sense of security and can ease the pangs of separating.

❖ Be prepared for an increase in separation anxiety when your child is faced with a major change, such as a move to a new home, the arrival of a new sibling, or the start of child-care. Provide her with extra attention, comfort, and reassurance.

❖ Tell your child when you will see her again, in terms she can understand: after her nap; when grandma picks her up, etc.

❖ Describe a routine event that you and she can look forward to doing when you return, such as reading a book together or playing with a favorite toy.

❖ Give your child a familiar or comforting object to keep – such as a family photograph or her favorite blanket – until you return.

Be patient, and allow your older baby to go through this stage at her own pace. Separation anxiety eventually passes.

on my way

18 - 36 months

—— • ——

Your bundle of joy is no longer a vulnerable infant. He is moving out and away, into the world on his own two feet. Although you are still the center of his universe, your role changes to meet his needs as he becomes more independent each day.

—— • ——

developmental milestones

DEVELOPMENTAL MILESTONES ARE THOSE IMPORTANT "FIRSTS" that let you know how quickly your toddler is growing. At this stage of his development, your child's main goal is to become independent. Although he is learning to do many things for himself, he still needs your constant loving care and guidance.

MILESTONE CONCERNS

Do not be surprised during this stage of your toddler's growth if he sometimes REGRESSES – that is, temporarily goes back to an earlier stage of development. The reason for this is simple. Your child is trying to master so many challenging new tasks at the same time that he often needs to "take a break." At this age, he is acquiring skills in four distinct areas: motor skills (physical movement and control), language skills (understanding and communicating with others through words and gestures), social-emotional skills (interacting and cooperating with others), and cognitive skills (learning and comprehending new concepts).

If your toddler is working very hard at mastering one skill, he may regress in another area – just to give himself a "rest." For example, if he is focused on learning to walk, he may not learn any new words for several weeks. Similarly, if he is toilet-trained – but putting all his energy into learning to ride a tricycle – he may "forget" his toilet training and wet his pants.

18 to 24 months

Your baby is now an active toddler. He learns to run, walks up and down stairs with support, and jumps with both feet. He understands complex sentences, uses words to tell you what he wants, and can wait for his needs to be met. He recognizes himself in pictures, uses his own name, and begins to combine two or three words into phrases. By two years of age, he has at least a 20-word vocabulary. He eats with a spoon and handles a cup quite well. He points to two or three body parts when you ask him to, tries to copy what you draw with a pencil, and frequently mimics doing household chores. He plays side by side with other children and helps put away toys when asked.

24 to 36 months

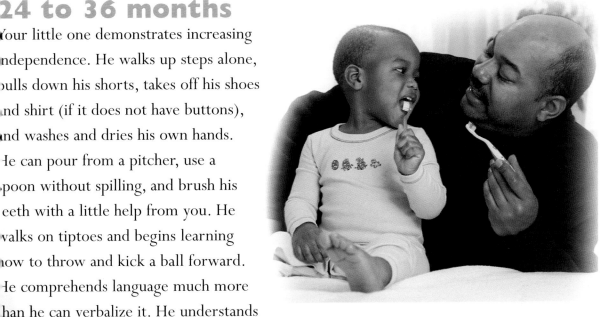

Your little one demonstrates increasing independence. He walks up steps alone, pulls down his shorts, takes off his shoes and shirt (if it does not have buttons), and washes and dries his own hands. He can pour from a pitcher, use a spoon without spilling, and brush his teeth with a little help from you. He walks on tiptoes and begins learning how to throw and kick a ball forward. He comprehends language much more than he can verbalize it. He understands verbs such as "eating," "running," and "sleeping," and differences in size, such as "big" and "little." He can identify one or more colors. He uses short sentences, begins to ask questions, and can hold up the right number of fingers when asked his age. He can build a tower of six blocks, joins in singing familiar songs, and listens when you read a simple book to him. He can anticipate the need to have a bowel movement, and can learn to use the toilet if you work with him.

Between two and three years old, your toddler imitates the actions of adults and older children. The many things he is learning now build on each other to help him become stronger, more alert, and better able to communicate.

WHEN TO CALL THE PEDIATRICIAN

Call your pediatrician immediately if your child has a fever over 102°F, a cough that does not go away, trouble breathing, cries constantly, or is in severe pain (especially in the head or chest). You should also consult your pediatrician if your toddler is not walking or saying a few words by 18 months of age.

Schedule well-child checkups at 18 and 24 months of age to ensure your toddler is healthy and growing steadily.

18 THROUGH 36 MONTHS

transitions

THE CHANGE FROM ONE EVENT TO ANOTHER IS KNOWN AS A TRANSITION. Moving from one activity to another can be a real challenge for your toddler. For example, if she is playing, and suddenly you tell her to stop and clean up, she may not react positively! Easing transitions for your child will help her adjust to changes with less stress.

temperament and transitions

TEMPERAMENT PLAYS A ROLE IN HOW easily a child makes transitions. Some children adapt to change and do not require several reminders or a lot of advance notice. The toddler who shows high adaptability has an easier time with transitions, but even she may have an occasional "bad" day.

Other children need more advance notice and still others need constant reminding. You should take your child's unique temperament into account when developing transition strategies. For example, if your toddler is easily distracted by sudden changes, plan extra time in the morning to get her dressed and ready for the day. A few minutes can make all the difference.

BEWARE THE BOOGEYMAN!

Scare tactics should never be used to motivate children. Saying things like "You'd better hurry or the boogeyman's going to get you!" or threatening to leave your child if she does not come along, may work the first time – but do not work in the long run. Children trust their parents to take care of them: Threats compromise that trust. Telling your child that you are going to leave her may cause her to develop fears. Instead of using scare and threat tactics, encourage your child to cooperate with you and to develop the basics of time management. Teach her about teamwork.

A little information goes a long way when making transitions. If you simply explain what is going to "happen next," your child is more likely to go along with your plans.

preparing for a change

ELLING YOUR CHILD WHAT IS GOING TO
appen next really helps. Being made
ware that a change is going to take place
and having some time to prepare for it)
ives a toddler important information,
ffers her the opportunity to finish what
he is doing, and helps her feel considered
nd respected in the process.

Routines also help with transitions. If
our child understands that the evening
outine is dinner, bath time, stories, and
edtime, she may be less resistant to the
rocess of getting ready for bed.

TIPS FOR MAKING EASIER TRANSITIONS

Some transitions evoke stronger feelings than others – for parents and children alike. Leaving for child-care on Monday mornings, for example, is a common trigger for temper tantrums. Here are some tips that may help make these and other transitions easier:

❖ Tell your child what is going to happen so she knows what to expect next.

❖ Talk to your child at her eye level to ensure that she hears and understands you.

❖ Plan ahead. Give your child a 5- to 10-minute warning before making a change. Give yourself and your child enough time to do whatever is necessary beforehand, and then add a few extra minutes for "unexpected emergencies."

❖ Try "counting down" to help your child make a transition. For example, if you want your child to stop playing and get ready for dinner, start out by saying, "In five minutes, it will be time to eat dinner." At one minute remind your child again, "It's just about time. Just one minute more." The concept of time is difficult for small children to grasp, but they can begin to get the general idea of what "five minutes" or "one minute" means.

❖ Songs are a great way to make transitions. Children often seem to respond to songs about routines and tasks more than they do to verbal requests. One very popular song heard in many child-care settings is about clean-up time after play: "Clean up, clean up, everybody everywhere, everybody do your share, clean up, clean up."

❖ To ease transitions, give your child a few choices whenever possible. For example, ask her, "Would you like to take your bunny or your bear with us?" or "Do you want to have yogurt or a fruit roll-up for dessert?" These kinds of questions help your child begin to think about the day ahead, make mental transitions, and feel she has a little control over her world.

❖ Make car or bus rides fun. For example, you can say, "Let's go find some big trucks!" or "Let's go look for red cars!" This exercise also helps children learn to observe what is going on around them.

❖ Give your child a special blanket or well-loved toy to take to child-care so that she can have "a part of home" with her during the day. She can even get her special toy ready for the day, which in turn helps her to get ready.

sleep

To A TODDLER, GOING TO SLEEP MEANS SAYING GOOD-BYE TO, and letting go of, loved ones for awhile, which is why children this age naturally resist going to bed. A consistent bedtime routine helps your child understand when it is time to go to sleep for the evening. The comfort and reassurance of bedtime routines also teach your child that "good nights" are followed by "good mornings." As your child grows, these nightly rituals help him feel more comfortable and confident when handling other sleep issues, such as bad dreams or even moving to a "big bed."

HELPING A CHILD MOVE TO HIS OWN BED

❖ Prepare your child for the transition by reading him books about children who sleep in big beds.

❖ Let your child go with you to buy the bed or select the bedspread and sheets. New "big boy" pajamas might also add to the excitement.

❖ Put the new bed in his room – next to the crib (or your own bed, if that is where he has been sleeping). Consider using special bed rails to ensure he does not fall out.

❖ If he is anxious about the transition, let him "visit" the big bed during the day – to read or play on, or even to take a nap.

❖ When he is ready for the move, follow your usual bedtime routine and help him get settled into his new bed. If he is a little scared, you may want to sit next to him or just outside his room until he falls asleep.

❖ Be sure to praise him in the morning for sleeping all night long in his big bed. After a few successful nights, you can say "bye-bye" to the crib and remove it from the room.

moving to a "big bed"

MANY TWO-YEAR-OLDS — especially if they are closer to three years – actually look forward to "graduating" to a "big bed." Still other two- and three-year-olds strongly resist leaving the security of their cribs. A beloved bedtime routine may be disrupted when the time comes for your child to move to a big bed. Sleeping in a crib or with parents provides a certain sense of security, and the transition to a new bed can be frightening.

Follow your child's lead about making this big change – he is sure to send you cues about his readiness. Remember that patience, constant reassurance, and "taking it slow" are key to a successful transition.

help for crib-climbers

IF YOUR TODDLER STARTS climbing out of his crib, consider his physical safety first and foremost. Dismantle the crib and put it away, but leave the crib mattress on the floor. Put him to sleep on the mattress, but continue his bedtime routine as usual. Once he figures out that he can easily leave the mattress, you need to let him know that he should stay put and call you if he needs you. Reassure him that you will come to him right away — and be sure to do so if he calls.

Reading stories together is a favorite bedtime ritual for parents and children. Books with a repetitive storyline soothe your child and help him feel sleepy.

handling nightmares

ALMOST ALL CHILDREN HAVE NIGHTMARES from time to time. Because children have so little control over their lives, their fears and anxieties often overwhelm them and "come out" in the form of nightmares. Usually "bad dreams" are about monsters that feel real – and very scary – to a small child. Never ignore your child's night-mares. Because children are most frightened of being abandoned by the grown-ups they depend on, it becomes doubly important for you to go to your child and comfort him when he feels afraid. You can also help him learn to comfort himself. Try giving him a special stuffed animal – such as a teddy bear – and tell him that if he gets scared, he can hug the bear really tight and tell the bear how he feels.

CRIBS FOR TWO?

If you are expecting a new baby in a few months, and your toddler is sleeping in a crib, you may be wondering what type of sleeping arrange-ments you should make. If your two-year-old is looking forward to a "big boy" bed, take advantage of this great time to move him. Do it as soon as possible, so he has time to adjust to his new bed before the baby arrives. If he is hesitant, a second crib might be a good idea. Be sure to let him know he can move to a big bed when he is ready.

reflecting feelings

FROM A VERY EARLY AGE YOUR BABY LOOKS CLOSELY AT YOUR FACE to see your reactions to her behavior. She already knows when you are pleased or unhappy with her. Now, besides learning new words that name and describe things, your child is ready to learn the words for her feelings. What is going on inside your child is just as important as what is going on outside. Young children need to learn about the emotions they feel – and how to express those feelings. You can help by giving your toddler the words she needs to express her emotions – this is called REFLECTING FEELINGS.

WHEN YOUR YOUNG CHILD GETS HURT . . .

How do you react when your child gets hurt? Often parents say, "Oh, it's alright. You're okay." But this reaction does not let the child know that you understand she is hurting. This may be very confusing for a young child. Next time your child gets hurt, acknowledge the pain while providing comfort. You might say, "Ouch! I know that hurts. Here, let's rub it – maybe that will help make it feel better." Recognizing your child's pain is very comforting to her. Rather than prolonging the incident, it actually helps her recover more quickly and move on to another activity.

Your child and you will share many joys and tears throughout your lives. Your relationship is strengthened by your ability to share and accept each other's many feelings.

how to reflect feelings

REFLECTING FEELINGS IS EASY WHEN your child is in a playful, happy mood. You might say, "You are such a happy girl!" Reflecting your child's feelings is more difficult, however, when she is experiencing something painful, such as anger or sadness. For example, if your child is crying, you might say, "Are you sad?" or "Are you angry?"– and then encourage her to talk about her feelings.

Looking at pictures and reading stories together is another way to encourage her. For example, you can talk about why a baby in a picture is smiling or crying. You might ask, "What happened to the baby? Why is she sad?" Or, "That little girl looks frustrated. See her face? What happened?" The more words your child learns for her feelings, the sooner she learns to express her inner feelings to you.

reflecting frustration

Talking about your own feelings encourages your child to talk about hers. You can let her know when you are feeling sad, tired, or frustrated. She learns that you have feelings, too, and notices the things you do to help yourself feel better. For example, you might say to her, "Mommy is tired now. Let's clean up the toys and sit down to read some books."

CHILDREN OFTEN CRY WHEN THEY are tired or frustrated. If you provide your child with words for her feelings, eventually she learns to tell you what is bothering her, instead of crying. For example, you may notice that your child is frustrated because she cannot open her juice box. You might say, "That looks hard to open. It's frustrating when you are trying hard to do something and it just doesn't work. Do you need some help?" When children learn to use words to

communicate their needs, they also learn that they can control their surroundings in a positive way. This is a big step towards growing up and becoming independent.

When you do not know exactly why your child is frustrated or fussy, just make your best guess. Cuddling with your child, or moving her to a quiet spot, may be enough to calm her. You are also showing her that she can remove herself from frustrating situations in the future.

respecting "contrary" feelings

SOMETIMES IT IS APPROPRIATE FOR you to acknowledge your child's feelings while expecting her to behave differently. For instance, she may say, "I don't want to clean up my toys. I'm angry." You can recognize her feelings and still require her to comply with your rules: "I know you don't feel like cleaning up all these blocks. It's a big mess, isn't it? When you finish the job, you can go outside to play." In another instance, your child may resist getting dressed and reach out to hit you. You might reply, "Hitting is not allowed in this family. You can talk to me when you are angry." Take your child's hand in yours and look directly at her, saying, "Tell me what's wrong. Are you

angry?" Even if your child is not able to answer at this point, you are still providing words for her feelings. Later, she will learn how to use those words to describe her feelings on her own.

praiseandencouragement

PRAISE AND ENCOURAGEMENT ARE IMPORTANT TOOLS for building your child's self-esteem, motivating her to learn, and reinforcing positive behavior. However, praise and encouragement are not the same things. PRAISE is about approval. ENCOURAGEMENT is about motivation. Learning when to praise or to encourage, and understanding the differen[t] effects of each approach, are essential to raising a healthy, independent child.

HOW TO ENCOURAGE YOUR CHILD

Encouraging your child in the right way, so that she finds the motivation within herself to keep on learning, working, and persisting (even when the going gets tough), takes some practice. Here are a few tips for giving valuable encouragement:

❖ Acknowledge hard work or positive behavior with precise, enthusiastic statements ("You rode your bike all the way across the playground!" or "You worked hard on your painting!"), but avoid comparisons or judgements ("You're the best bike rider in the neighborhood!" or "You painted the prettiest picture at child-care.")

❖ Focus on the behavior or process ("You used all the colors to paint your picture!"), not only on the outcome ("What a beautiful picture!").

❖ Use simple and sincere statements, and only comment on what you observe. For example, you might say to your toddler, "You are pouring your own juice!"

the difference between praise and encouragement

WHEN YOU PRAISE YOUR TODDLER for doing something, you are letting her know that you approve of her actions and that they please you. When she learns what makes you happy she is more likely to repeat the pleasing behavior. When you acknowledge how hard your child is working at a particular task, you are encouraging and motivating her to stick with it. At the same time she learns that she can please herself (with persistence and hard work), her self-esteem also gets a boost, making her more likely to tackle greater challenges.

For example, imagine your three-year-old is sitting next to you, working very hard to put together a new puzzle. She fits the first few pieces together easily, but has a difficult time finishing the puzzle, gets frustrated, and starts to give up. You might say, "That's great! I like the way you put those pieces

together." She enjoys the praise and is happy that she pleased you, but she is not motivated to continue working on the puzzle. On the other hand, when she starts to give up, you could say, "You can do it. Keep trying. You'll get it!" You are encouraging her to stay motivated and keep working until she succeeds. When she does "get it," you might then tell her, "You worked so hard to finish that. You must feel so proud." This puts the focus on her work and accomplishment, instead of on pleasing you.

Encouraging your child to develop an "I think I can" attitude helps her negotiate life's challenges with more confidence.

When your child is learning a new task, stay close by, ask questions, listen carefully but let her do things by herself. This is the best way to encourage her to stay motivate[d] and keep trying.

encourage more, praise less . . .

THE OLD SAYING, "A LITTLE PRAISE GOES A LONG way," may be true after all. Recent literature recommends that parents and caregivers use encouragement rather than praise — or rewards like stickers and gold stars — to inspire children to discover for themselves the values of hard work, persistence, positive behavior, and self-motivation. Children love to be praised, of course, and praise can be very affirming — but not when it is given too frequently. In fact, according to early childhood expert Lillian Katz, praise loses its value when its used too often, and may even be ignored by children as "empty talk." Save your praise for meaningful moments between you and your child, when she can really "hear" and appreciate it.

aggression**and**
self-discipline

D O NOT BE SURPRISED IF THE SWEET BABY who lay so peacefully in your arms when he was 6 months old becomes quite aggressive between 18 and 36 months. Aggressive words (saying hurtful things, using inappropriate language, and screaming) together with aggressive behavior (hitting, biting, shoving, kicking, and pinching) are common at this age. Helping your young child control his words and behavior can be challenging. Understanding why he acts aggressively can assist you in helping him learn self-discipline.

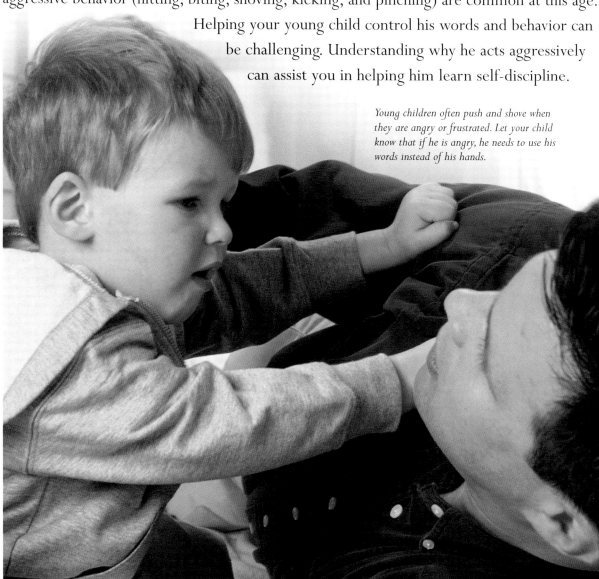

Young children often push and shove when they are angry or frustrated. Let your child know that if he is angry, he needs to use his words instead of his hands.

understanding aggressive behavior

CHILDREN BEHAVE AGGRESSIVELY FOR various reasons. They may not yet have the verbal skills to express their feelings. They may have limited social skills. They are experimenting with how their words and actions affect others (that is, experimenting with "cause and effect"). They may be imitating the language and behavior of others.

Verbal skills. Your toddler is just learning to use words to describe his feelings. When he cannot do something, such as zipping up his jacket, for example, he may become angry or frustrated. Because he cannot express those feelings in words, he may "act out" the feelings by screaming, crying, or throwing things. He may even say, "I hate you!" *What you can do:* Teach your child the words that describe his feelings. For example, if he is struggling with the zipper on his jacket, you might say, "I can see that you are frustrated with that zipper. Would you like some help?" Or if he says, "I hate you," you can say, "It's okay to tell me you are angry or frustrated, but it's not okay to say you hate me."

Social skills. Your child is just beginning to socialize with others and he may hit, pinch, shove, or bite when he is angry or frustrated with another child or an adult. *What you can do:* If your toddler hits, for example, you can hold his hands and say, "Hands are for loving, not hurting. If you are angry, use your words." Never hit (pinch, shove, or bite) back, and never shame your toddler ("You are such a bad boy!").

Sometimes it is hard to tell if children are hurting each other or "just playing." Be ready to redirect them to a safer activity if necessary.

Cause and effect. Your toddler is just discovering how to use his body to make things happen. For example, he may seem to delight in "purposely" breaking toys or pulling the cat's tail. Chances are, however, that he simply does not know his own strength and needs to be redirected. *What you can do:* If your child accidentally hurts pets or breaks things, show him how to use his hands gently to pet an animal or handle an object. Practice with him, and then praise him, when he gets it right.

Imitation. It is natural for your child to imitate your words, actions, and reactions, so you may want to take a look at your own behavior. Do you spank your toddler? Hit the dog? Curse? Scream or bang things when you are angry? *What you can do:* Monitor your own language and behavior, and only use those words and actions that you would want your toddler to use. When you're upset or disappointed, use "your words" to tell your child how angry or frustrated you are. Instead of spanking or screaming at your child, use positive discipline techniques, such as setting limits and redirection. For serious problems, use the "thinking chair" (see sidebar on page 75).

learning self-discipline

IF YOU APPROACH BEHAVIOR problems with patience and a positive attitude, your child will eventually become self-disciplined. She wants to please you, even when it comes to learning self-control. The following techniques are especially useful.

Using repetition. You may need to repeat rules, instructions, and explanations many times – over a period of time – before your toddler "gets the message" about unacceptable behavior. For example, it may take her months to learn how to "use her hands gently." It is unrealistic to expect your child to learn and remember a new task or skill right away.

Avoiding shame. Avoid shaming your child when she makes mistakes. Instead, take her aside, away from others, and quietly explain what the mistake was and what behavior you would like to see instead.

Focusing on positive discipline techniques. Positive discipline techniques, such as encourage- ment, reflecting feelings, redirection, childproofing, and setting limits, help your child learn

self-discipline. These techniques work because they build self-esteem and teach your child what acceptable behavior is.

The best method for helping your child learn self-discipline is by example: Behave the way you want her to behave. Add in positive discipline techniques and lots of love, and she will be on her way to becoming a happy, healthy person.

DISCIPLINE TECHNIQUE: THE "THINKING CHAIR"

The "thinking chair" technique not only stops unacceptable behavior, but also helps your child learn how to handle similar situations in the future. Follow these tips to use the "thinking chair" successfully. (This technique works best for children who are at least 30 months old.)

❖ Decide what behaviors warrant a visit to the thinking chair. Choose only one or two behaviors that are totally unacceptable in your home, such as hitting and biting.

❖ Tell your child that if she hits or bites, she will spend time in the

thinking chair, which should be in a quiet part of the home.

❖ When your child hits someone (to use hitting as an example), tell her, "Hitting is against the rules. Let's spend some time in the thinking chair."

❖ Give the child a kitchen timer to hold and tell her, "When the timer goes off, I will talk to you about this soon. In the meantime, I want you to think about what happened and try to figure out what you can do the next time you are angry – instead of hitting." (Note: Do not set the timer

for more than one or two minutes.)

❖ Stay in the same room as your child, and when the time is up, ask her to talk to you about what happened. Ask her how she felt, how the other person might have felt, if she thinks she should apologize, and what she can do next time instead of hitting (for example, "use her words").

❖ Give her a hug and let her know she should be very proud of herself for thinking of new ways to handle her anger without hitting. Tell her she can go back to play.

tantrums

I F YOUR CHILD LOSES EMOTIONAL CONTROL to such a degree that he is reduced to prolonged screaming, whining, kicking, and hitting – and cannot be reasoned with – he is having a tantrum. Knowing that tantrums are common in young children does not make it easier to deal with them. Parents dread tantrums, especially because they often occur in public. Understanding why your child may have tantrums, and learning a few techniques for preventing and handling them, help minimize the occurence of these uncomfortable situations.

why tantrums happen

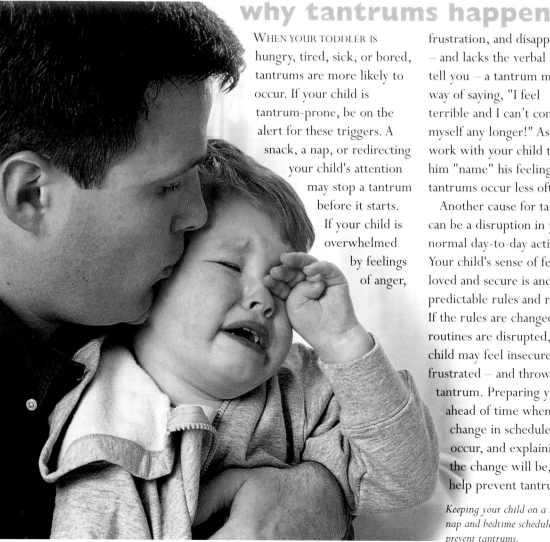

WHEN YOUR TODDLER IS hungry, tired, sick, or bored, tantrums are more likely to occur. If your child is tantrum-prone, be on the alert for these triggers. A snack, a nap, or redirecting your child's attention may stop a tantrum before it starts. If your child is overwhelmed by feelings of anger, frustration, and disappointment – and lacks the verbal skills to tell you – a tantrum may be his way of saying, "I feel terrible and I can't control myself any longer!" As you work with your child to help him "name" his feelings, tantrums occur less often.

Another cause for tantrums can be a disruption in your normal day-to-day activities. Your child's sense of feeling loved and secure is anchored in predictable rules and routines. If the rules are changed or routines are disrupted, your child may feel insecure and frustrated – and throw a tantrum. Preparing your child ahead of time when a change in schedule will occur, and explaining what the change will be, can help prevent tantrums.

Keeping your child on a regular nap and bedtime schedule helps prevent tantrums.

how to handle tantrums

THE MOST IMPORTANT RULE ABOUT handling tantrums is **never give in**! No matter how humiliated your child's tantrum makes you feel, giving in to his demands — for a candy bar in a supermarket, for example — sends him a disastrous message: If you throw a tantrum, you will get what you want. He may stop his embarrassing behavior for the moment, but the next time he wants something, he is more likely to have another tantrum. Instead of giving in to your child, use one of these techniques:

Ignore the tantrum completely. Do not talk to or look at your child. Walk a few feet away and continue with whatever you were doing before (for example, grocery shopping). If you are in public, try to ignore the stares of bystanders — as difficult as that may be. Attention will only "feed" a tantrum ("Hey, look at me!"). Ignoring your child's behavior, however, may "starve" the tantrum and make it stop more quickly. ("Nobody is paying attention. This isn't working.")

Remove your child from the scene. Calmly tell him you will wait for him to finish having his tantrum, so you can continue your shopping.

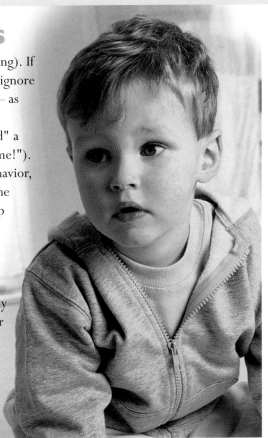

As soon as your child stops a tantrum, praise him for regaining control.

PREVENTING TANTRUMS

Tantrums can happen anywhere, but public tantrums are the most embarrassing. Here we use the classic "supermarket tantrum" as an example, but you can modify these tips to help prevent other types of tantrums.

Before leaving for the store:

❖ Set specific guidelines for your child about how to behave at the supermarket. For example, tell him also that he can pick out one treat, and that if he has a tantrum, he will not be able to go with you to the store next time.

❖ Pack a special snack bag for him.

❖ Prepare a list of the grocery items you need.

❖ Go to a store you are familiar with so you can find things quickly.

Note: If your child is hungry, tired, or sick, leave him at home with another adult or a babysitter.

At the store:

❖ Let your child eat the snack you brought.

❖ Ask him to help you pick out items.

❖ Talk to him and explain what foods you are buying and why.

❖ If he asks for an item and you do not want to purchase it, you might say, "Oh, I know that looks great. I would like to have it, too! But we can't buy that today."

❖ Keep moving! Try to finish shopping as quickly as possible.

❖ Pay for your items at the candy-free checkout lane — if your supermarket has one.

play

A T THIS AGE PLAY IS YOUR CHILD'S "WORK." Through it she learns what nothing else can teach her. For example, when she's playing in the sandbox, she learns that wet sand holds its shape longer than dry sand, and that certain materials – such as grass or ice – feel different on her feet than they do on her tummy. Physical play is particularly important for your toddler because it exercises both her muscles and her mind. Active games such as hide-and-seek, throwing a ball, stacking blocks, or just crawling fast keep your child in shape. These activities also help set up good fitness habits for life.

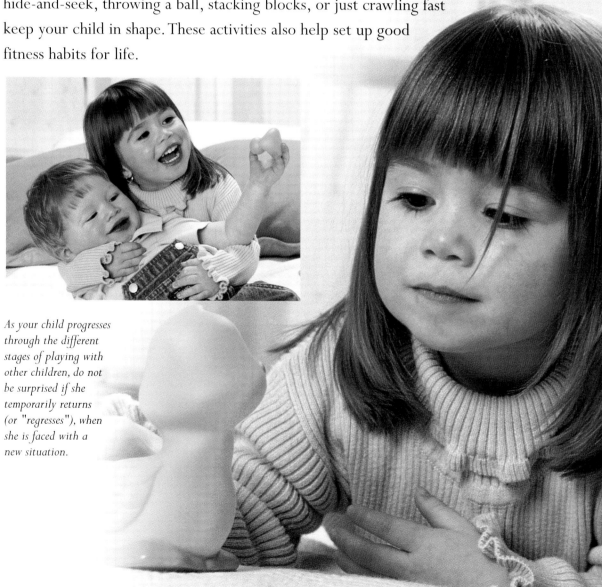

As your child progresses through the different stages of playing with other children, do not be surprised if she temporarily returns (or "regresses"), when she is faced with a new situation.

PLAYING WITH SIBLINGS AND OTHER CHILDREN

———— • ————

Playing with other children, including brothers and sisters, is more challenging for your toddler than playing with you or other caregivers. You are tuned in to her personality and style of play, and you have developed a comfortable give-and-take with her. For example, she shares toys and "takes turns" with you during play. But your child will not be able to play with children in the same way as she does with you for some time. Instead, she learns to play in specific stages.

❖ Parallel play occurs when children play alongside one another and share toys in a limited fashion. This type of play may begin as early as 18 months, but usually starts at 24 months. There may be fleeting contact between the children – that is, your child may actively seek involvement with another child – but the contact is so brief that there is really no time for the other child to respond.

❖ Rigid contact during play soon follows and involves simple, repeated interactions. Your child may seek another child's participation in a play activity, but in a specific manner, with no room for compromise. For example, she might ask another child to "fill" her toy car with "gas." As long as the other child agrees to do exactly this, play continues. If the other child does not comply, or wants to do something else, play ends.

❖ Associative play is a more complex and interactive play stage where children are able to "share" a play theme for a short time. Generally, this does not begin until your child is at least three-and-a-half years old.

Allow your child to attempt to do as much of a new activity as she can by herself – even if it is a difficult one, such as learning to blow bubbles. It is also a good idea to teach her to clean up after one activity before going on to a new one.

SHARING WITH OTHER CHILDREN

Although most parents expect their two- and three-year-old children to share, child experts say this is an unreasonable expectation. Your toddler is naturally possessive. She has learned the concept of "mine," and it is extremely difficult for her to share with others.

There are several things you can do, however, to help her begin to understand the concept of sharing:

❖ When she is playing with another child, provide two similar items for each child.

❖ If a friend is coming over to play, decide beforehand which toys will be shared, and then put the rest of the toys away.

❖ Show your child and her friend how to take turns if they fight over the same toy.

❖ Suggest a change of scenery: Take the children outside, so they can play together, rather than focussing on a toy or game.

testing the parent-child connection through play

DESPITE YOUR CHILD'S GROWING independence, her connection with you and other caregivers is still of utmost importance to her. She will test how solid this connection is in a uniquely playful – and sometimes alarming – way. When you are in public – for example, in the park, a playground, or a mall – she may sometimes take off on her own and walk or run away from you. If you are in a safe environment, where she really cannot get away from you, do not stop her. She will soon stop herself and look back at you. Watch her, wave, but stay where you are. She'll run on a little further, then stop again. She may repeat this behavior

several times. Just when you think she's gone too far, she will turn around and come running back to you, relieved that you are still there, where she left you.

Child development experts call this behavior "CHECKING BACK." This is an important way for your child to learn about the stability and security of your relationship. She is reassured that you will always be there for her. This is the same experience she had as an older baby when she played peekaboo with you and discovered, with great excitement, that you were still there – behind the blanket or the chair – every time.

languageandlearning

Y OUR CHILD IS NOW EXPLORING THE WORLD in a very active way. She learns a great deal through every interaction with her environment and with her playmates and older siblings. She also continues to learn from the important adults in her life, especially from you – her first and best teacher.

RAISING A BILINGUAL CHILD

If you are raising your toddler in a bilingual household, you may be concerned that she is not learning to speak as rapidly as you wish. Generally, a child who is exposed consistently to two languages takes longer to express herself in either language, because she has a lot more information to process. This is normal. However, if you have any concerns about your child's language development, it is always a good idea to have her hearing checked, especially if she has had repeated ear infections.

When you know that her hearing is not the problem, chances are that she comprehends much more than he is able to express verbally. For example, you can tell by her actions if she understands simple commands, such as, "Go get your shoes." or "Lets eat some crackers."

Some language experts suggest having one family member speak only one language to the child and another person speak only the other language. The key is to be patient. In time, and at her own pace, your child will begin speaking both languages fluently.

using the everyday world to learn

AS YOUR TODDLER'S FIRST TEACHER you can use her everyday world as a classroom. The following activities offer valuable learning experiences.

When you are driving in the car or riding on the bus, point to things you see out the window and name them. Your child will begin to learn that there are names for everything.

When you shop at the supermarket, talk about the things you are buying. Let your child watch as you mark off items on your shopping list. Read the signs in the market out loud, to show her that reading goes on everywhere. Use items in the store to talk about concepts like size and weight, using words such as "bigger" and "smaller," "heavy" and "light."

The playground is a particularly good place to teach your child about concepts such as "inside" and "outside," "up" and "down." Climbing in and out of, and over and under, playground equipment is an excellent way for your child to learn about directions.

Your child will learn from making messes, too. Playing in water, dirt, and sand allows her to learn about different sensations and textures. She will also enjoy burying toys in the sand and finding them again. At first, your child may not like getting dirty, and she may need some encouragement. Every child has his or her own level of sensitivity, so respect your child's needs and temperament.

Making bath time a part of your child's daily routine is especially enjoyable for her because she knows she will get your undivided attention. Watch her play with objects that float and sink. Let her name parts of her body as you wash them. At this age it is natural for boys and girls to explore their genitals. This curiosity is part of how children develops a unique self-image. By now, your child sees herself as a separate physical being. Looking in the mirror, she knows she is looking at herself.

et your child take the lead at playtime. Watch to see if she
acks the blocks or lines them up. As she gets older, it's a
ood idea to wait and see how she invites you into her games.

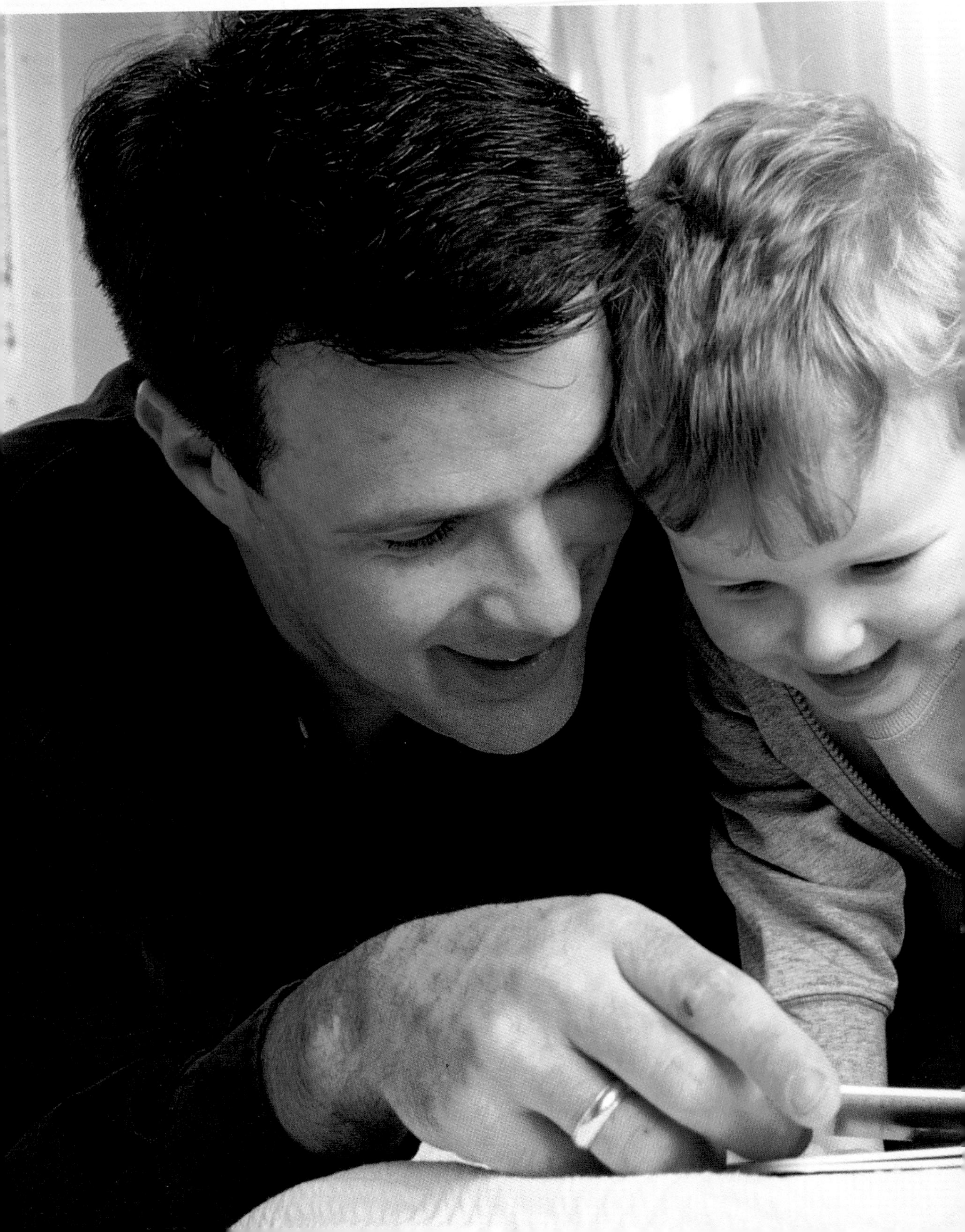

Reading to your child is always a good idea. Sometimes he will be patient as you read every word on each page. Other times he will get just as much satisfaction simply from looking at the pictures in a favorite book with you.

LANGUAGE DEVELOPMENT

Your child is learning new words every day from his interactions with you and others, but he will not verbalize all that he hears right away. Instead, his language development progresses on two levels.

❖ **Receptive language** begins to develop first. This is the language your child receives and understands through listening. At this stage, it is helpful to use short sentences to explain and describe things, so that your toddler can learn and understand new words and concepts. You can also use your tone of voice and gestures to give more meaning to your words. For example, you might say, "See the cat? She feels soft. Let's touch her gently," using a soft tone of voice and using your hands to show what "touching gently" means. Your toddler then "receives" your words on many levels at the same time.

❖ **Expressive language** develops as your child hears the same words repeated many times and begins to express them verbally. During this stage of language development, it is important to give your child plenty of "thinking time" before he responds to a question. Wait for his answer. He may first respond with a look or a gesture. This is also communication, so acknowledge it. The words will follow.

Listening to stories and songs on tape will also encourage language development, and delight your child at the same time. He will also learn a good deal from just looking at the pictures in a favorite book with you. Books provide the same pictures in the same order each time you go through them. This predictability pleases your child, because he can look forward to what's coming next. The pictures can also be used as learning tools. For example, you might ask your toddler to touch a bunny's ear in a book, then touch his ear, and then your ear. This helps him make connections between the things he sees in books and the things he sees in his life. This is true learning! And if he wants to turn the page before you have finished reading all the words, that's okay too. Just adjust to his speed.

toiletteaching

A S SOON AS YOUR TODDLER HAS HER FIRST BIRTHDAY, friends and relatives may start telling you that it is time for her to get out of diapers and start using the potty. The truth is, i is your child who ultimately decides when she is ready. Most children learn to use the toile between the ages of two and four. The age your child learns – within that range – is not important. Relax! Just as she learned to sit up, hold a spoon, and walk, your child will also learn to use the potty.

SIGNS OF TOILET READINESS

Your child is ready to start learning how to use the toilet when she shows two or more of these signs of readiness:

❖ Stays dry for several hours at a time, or wakes up dry in the morning or after naps.

❖ Has the ability to let others know what she wants and needs.

❖ Wants to sit on the toilet and sometimes even urinates or has a bowel movement.

❖ Begins to tell you when she is "wet" or "dry," and understands the difference between the two.

❖ Tells you she wants to wear "big girl" pants.

❖ Shows an interest in how others (including pets!) urinate or have bowel movements.

❖ Can put on and remove simple items of clothing.

preparing to toilet teach your child

THERE IS NO ONE "RIGHT WAY" TO help teach your child to use the potty. The best method might be to approach teaching her to use the toilet in much the same way she has learned to do other things. For example, if your child is very sociable, she may enjoy having the potty in the center of things in the house, perhaps even in the living room. Once she gets used to the idea of using the potty, you can move the potty chair into the bathroom.

Watch your child for signs of readiness (see sidebar), but let her tell you, in her own way, that she is ready for this new endeavor.

Most experts recommend that you first let your child gain control of her bowels, then work on learning to use the toilet to urinate. The reason for this is that there is more warning time for bowel movements. By the time a child tells you that she needs to urinate, however, it is often too late. Remember, your child's goal is to be successful in learning how to use the toilet – and to feel good about learning to do things for herself.

MAKING TOILET TEACHING FUN

❖ Put a drop or two of blue food coloring in the toilet. When your child urinates in the toilet, she will be delighted to watch the water turn green!

❖ Let your child "play" with the potty training idea by using a doll. She can place the doll on the potty and pretend the doll is using the toilet. She can even play the role of "parent," praising and encouraging the doll for her efforts.

❖ If the weather is warm, bring your child's potty outdoors and let her go bare-bottomed while playing outside. She can sit on the potty whenever she wishes and accidents will not be a big deal

teaching your child to use the toilet

NOW IS WHEN YOUR CHILD WILL really rely on your encouragement. Remember to go slowly and be patient and flexible. Follow these guidelines for successful toilet teaching.

Buy a potty chair and tell your child, "This is your potty chair.

Let's put it right next to the big potty. Whenever you want, it's here for you to use." Some parents even encourage their child to carry the potty with them throughout the house, so that when she has the urge to use the potty, it's right there.

Allow your child to sit on the potty whenever she wants. You can use a special potty seat that fits over the toilet and allows your toddler to sit comfortably. Or you can use a freestanding potty chair. Your child will quickly let you know which one she prefers.

Encourage any attempt your child makes to use the toilet. Even if she tells you she has to go, and you discover she has already urinated, turn it into a learning opportunity. You might say, "You didn't quite make it in time. You'll get it before too long."

Start little boys out by sitting them down on the toilet. Once they get used to urinating in the toilet this way, then they can try it standing up.

When accidents happen, remain calm. Let your child help with cleaning up and changing into dry clothes as much as she can. The goal is independence and feeling good about herself.

Consider using training pants. Diapers work so well today that toddlers often cannot feel when they are wet. Training pants and other pull-up type pants allow your child to feel the wetness of urine, and she can easily take them on and off.

Be prepared for an "accident" whenever your child's regular routines are disrupted. The arrival of a new sibling, a move to a new house, or any other major change can bring about a temporary setback.

A favorite book to look at during potty time helps her relax while she gains new control of her body.

THINGS TO AVOID WHILE TOILET TEACHING

❖ Punishing your child for "accidents."

❖ Forcing your child to sit for long periods of time on the potty.

❖ Making your child sit on the potty if she is upset about the process.

❖ Comparing your child to other children or to siblings.

developing**empathy**

E MPATHY IS THE ABILITY TO UNDERSTAND and be sensitive to the feelings and experiences of other people. Statements such as, "I am sorry you are upset," "I understand," and "How can I help?" all reflect the capacity to empathize. While your young child is probably not quite able to make such statements now, you may notice that some of her actions reflect these caring thoughts. For example, has your toddler ever softly patted the back of another crying child? "Just happened" to give you a kiss when you needed it most? Cried over a sick or injured pet and tried to "make it better"? These are all ways she expresses empathy, one of the most important emotional qualities you can encourage in your child. Empathy is the foundation of all good relationships and of a healthy society.

Gently stroking her mother's forehead, this child shows that she has already learned something about empathy.

helping your child develop empathy

EMPATHY HELPS YOUR CHILD BETTER understand and develop strong connections to family and friends. She will also feel good about caring for and trying to help others. Encourage your child to develop empathy by using the "golden rule": "Treat others the way you would like to be treated."

You are the center of your child's world. Everything you do and say makes an impression on her. Treat your child the way you would want her to treat you and others. If you want her to be polite, say "please" and "thank you" to her. If you want her to do nice things for other people, talk about and show her how you care for others. If you want her to be able to comfort others, hug and kiss your child when she is sad or hurt. In other words, behave the way you want your child to behave.

Encourage your child to help care for other family members. A child who is two and a half to three years old can help an adult care for an elderly grandparent, a disabled child, or a newborn baby. For example, if you are changing the baby's diaper, you can tell your child, "The baby would sure be happy with a clean diaper. Do you know anyone who could get one for her?" When the older child brings you the diaper, you can say, "The baby is so happy now with a clean diaper. Thank you so much for helping her feel better!"

Be sure not to make these tasks into responsibilities or chores. Most children this age will want to help naturally, especially if the parent uses praise and encouragement.

TEACHING EMPATHY FOR PEOPLE WHO ARE "DIFFERENT"

Talk about differences in eye color, hair color, skin color, size, and shape. After discussing differences, ask your child how all people are the same. For example, you might point out that all people have heads and brains, or that even though people look different, they all have feelings inside.

Above all, never miss an opportunity to tell your child that you love her, and to give her lots of hugs and kisses. Children who feel loved learn to love and care for others.

ABOUT HITTING

If your child hits another child, it is better to help her understand how the other child feels, rather than to punish her – for two reasons. First, punishment may make your child angry and resentful, and she will not be in the mood to care about anyone else's feelings. Second, if she doesn't learn how her actions affect others, she is more likely to hit again. Ask your child specific questions, such as "How would you feel if someone hit you? How do you think your friend felt when you hit him? What can you do to help him feel better? What can you do next time you feel like hitting?" Learning and thinking about how others feel when they are hurt, and relating it to how your child feels, will help her develop empathy.

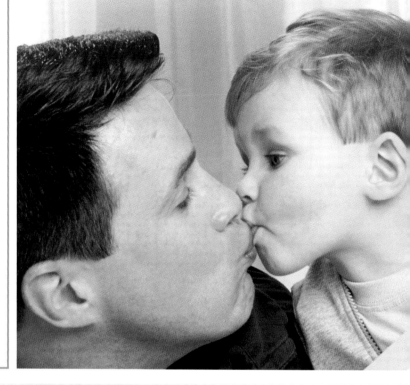

Your child learns to love and care for others by how he is treated. Lots of hugs and kisses produce good feelings all around!

HANDLING DIFFICULT QUESTIONS ABOUT DISABILITIES

What can you do when your child sees a differently-abled person – such as a man with one arm – points at him, and loudly says, "Mommy, what's wrong with that man?" Instead of focusing on your embarrassment, use the situation to help your child learn empathy for people who appear to be "different."

Quietly take your child aside and calmly explain, "That man may have had a disease or an accident. Or he might have been born with one arm." You can then ask your child the following questions and give her time to respond.

❖ "That man may look different to you on the outside, but how do you think he feels on the inside when people point at him and ask loud questions?"

❖ "How would you feel if people pointed at and asked loud questions about you?"

❖ "Next time you see someone who you think is very different, what could you do instead of pointing at him and asking loud questions?"

At the same time you can use this opportunity to help your child notice things that might be strong, positive, or "usual" about someone with a disability. For example, he or she may have children, drive a car, and hold a job. It's important to get across the idea that people with disabilities are not necessarily defined by them.

resources

BOOKS FOR CHILDREN

BIRTH TO 9 MONTHS

Baby's Colors, Mommy & Me, and *Daddy & Me* by Neil Ricklin, Simon & Schuster.

Touch & Feel Puppy, DK Publishing.

Duck is Dirty and other books by Satoshi Kitamura.

9 TO 18 MONTHS

Goodnight Moon by Margaret Wise Brown, Harper Festival/Harper and Row.

Touch and Feel Farm, Touch and Feel Wild Animals, and other *Touch and Feel* books by DK Publishing.

Firehouse Company No. 1: A Day in the Life of a Firehouse by Peter Lippman, Workman.

18 TO 36 MONTHS

The Berenstain Bears Inside, Outside, Upside Down by Stan and Jan Berenstain, Random House.

Tickle, Tickle and Clap Hand, by Helen Oxenbury, Simon & Schuster.

It Looked Like Spilt Milk by Charles G. Shaw, Harper Collins.

Chicka Chicka Boom Boom by John Archambault, Simon & Schuster.

Good Night Gorilla by Peggy Rathman, Penguin Putnam.

Jamberry by Bruce Degan, Harper Festival, a division of Harper Collins.

Peter's Chair by Ezra Jack Keats, Puffin Books.

Brown Bear, Brown Bear, What Do You see?, The Very Hungry Caterpillar, and other books by Eric Carle, Henry Holt.

BOOKS TO ENCOURAGE EMPATHY

Mama, If You Had a Wish by Jeanne Modesitt, Aladdin Paperbacks, Simon and Schuster.

Children Just Like Me by Barnabas and Anabel Kindersley, DK Publishing.

Feelings by Aliki, Mulberry Books.

The Berenstain Bears Forget Their Manners by Stan and Jan Berenstein, Random House.

Sometimes I Feel Like a Mouse by Jeanne Modesitt, Scholastic.

I Like Me by Nancy Carlson, Puffin Books.

BOOKS FOR PARENTS AND CAREGIVERS

Babyhood: Stage by Stage, from Birth to Age Two: How Your Baby Develops Physically, Emotionally, Mentally, Revised 2nd Edition, by Penelope Leach, Knopf, 1983.

Different and Wonderful by Darlene Hopson and Derek S. Hopson, Fireside, 1992.

Touchpoints: Your Child's Emotional and Behavioral Development by T. Berry Brazelton, M.D., Perseus Press, 1994.

What to Expect the First Year and What to Expect the Toddler Years by Arlene Eisenberg, Heidi Murkoff, and Sandra Hathaway, Workman, 1996.

VIDEOS FOR PARENTS AND CAREGIVERS

The following videocassettes may be ordered from the *I Am Your Child* web site and are available in English and Spanish. Or telephone 1-888-447-3400 (English) or 1-800-861-2241 (Spanish).

Discipline: Teaching Limits with Love shows parents that setting limits is not punishment, but a loving way to teach children how to control their own behavior.

The First Years Last Forever summarizes the latest brain research related to child development and offers parents specific tips on building stronger bonds with their babies.

Quality Child Care discusses why choosing the right child care is one of the most important decisions parents make.

Ready to Learn explores how the emotional closeness and language experiences between you and your child are an important part of preparing him or her for later learning.

Safe from the Start shows parents and caregivers what to do to prevent serious childhood injuries.

Your Healthy Baby demonstrates how parents and caregivers can help their children establish healthy habits for a lifetime.

WEB SITES

www.iamyourchild.org
On its website, the *I Am Your Child* Foundation offers a wide variety of parenting resources – including information about its acclaimed videos.

www.lalecheleague.org
La Leche League is an international organization that assists new mothers with breast-feeding and other lactation issues.

www.nectas.unc.edu
The National Early Childhood Technical Assistance System's (NECTAS) web site provides information about the Individuals with Disabilities Education Act (IDEA) and about programs funded under IDEA, including the Program for Infants and Toddlers with Disabilities. It also provides online professional referrals by state, as well as referrals for military personnel living outside the U.S.

www.totalbabycare.com
Sponsored by the Pampers Parenting Institute, this web site is the home of "House Calls," where famed pediatrician T. Berry Brazelton answers

questions and offers advice about early childhood development from birth to 12 months old.

www.zerotothree.org
Zero to Three is a national nonprofit charitable organization whose aim is to strengthen and support families, communities, and healthcare practitioners in order to promote the healthy development of babies and toddlers. Their web site provides a variety of information about the link between nurturing and early child development.

ORGANIZATIONS

National Early Childhood Intervention care line: 1-800-250-2246
The Early Child Intervention (ECI) care line puts you in touch with an ECI program in your area. Public Law 105-17, also known as the Individuals with Disabilities Education Act (IDEA), provides early intervention programs to assist infants and toddlers with disabilities and their families. ECI programs checks children (birth through age three) suspected of delays in development, and provides needed services at no cost to the family.

La Leche League, 1-800-LALECHE (1-800-525-3243) is devoted to helping new mothers cope with breast-feeding and other lactation issues.

references

Albrecht, K., and Miller, L. G. (2000) *The Comprehensive Toddler Curriculum*. Beltsville, MD: Gryphon House.

Bell, S. M., and Salter Ainsworth, M. D. (1972) "Infant crying and maternal responsiveness." *Child Development* 43, 1171–1190.

Bos, Beverly (1983) *Before the Basics: Creating Conversations with Children*. Roseville, CA: Turn the Page Press.

Brazelton, T. B. (1987) *What Every Baby Knows*. New York: Ballantine Books.
—(1994) *Touchpoints: Your Child's Emotional and Behavioral Development*. Reading, MA: Addison-Wesley.
—(1992) "By learning baby's style, parents benefit" in *Families Today* special feature. *New York Times*.

Eisenberg, A., Murkoff, H. E., and Hathaway, S. E. (1989) *What to Expect the First Year*. New York: Workman.

Erikson, E. H. (1963) Childhood and Society. New York: W. W. Norton. Second edition.

Frankenburg, W., and Dodds, J. (1990/1993) *Your Child's Growth: Developmental Milestones*. American Academy of Pediatrics, Division of Publications, 141 Northwest Point Blvd., P. O. Box 927, Elk Grove Village, IL, 60009-0927.

Freedman, D. A. (1997) *On Infancy and Toddlerhood: An Elementary Textbook*. Madison, CT: International Universities Press.

The Children's Museum of Houston (2001) *Fun Shop: Activities for Birth – Three*.

Lakner, L. (2000) "What's so bad about praise?" *Houston Area Association for the Education of Young Children Advocate* 19 (3).

Leach, P. (1998) *Your Baby and Child: From Birth to Age Five*: 3rd Edition. New York: Alfred A. Knopf.

Linden, J., and Pearson, D. (1992) *Playing with Your Baby: Birth to Six Months*. Copyright Jill Linden, Ph.D., Grasonville, MD and Douglas Pearson, Ph.D., Wilmington, DE.
—(1993) *Playing with Your Baby: Six to Nine Months*. Copyright Jill Linden, Ph.D., Grasonville, MD and Douglas Pearson, Ph.D., Wilmington, DE.

Mahler, M. S. (1972) "Rapprochement Subphase of the Separation-Individuation Process." *Psychoanalytic Quarterly* 41(4): 487–506.

Mangin, M. C. (1998) "Praise: what does it accomplish?" *Dimensions of Early Childhood*. Summer/Fall 1998.

Miller, Karen (1985) *Ages and Stages*. Chelsea, MA: Telshare Publishing.

Neville, H., and Clark Johnson, D. (1998) *Temperament Tools: Working with Your Child's Inborn Traits*. Seattle: Parenting Press.

Parents as Teachers National Center, Inc., and Missouri Department of Elementary and Secondary Education (1993) "Understanding the difference between stranger anxiety and separation anxiety" in *Program Planning and Implementation Guide*, p. 137.

Perry, B. D (1996) "An interview with Dr. Bruce D. Perry, Director of the CIVITAS Child Trauma Programs." Interviewed by Lou Bank, 1996. Copyright Bruce D. Perry, M.D.

Satter, Ellyn (1983) *Child of Mine: Feeding With Love and Good Sense*. Palo Alto, CA: Bull Publishing, 1983.

Shick, L. (1998) *Understanding Temperament: Strategies for Creating Family Harmony*. Seattle: Parenting Press.

Whiteside, M. F., Busch, F., and Horner, T. From *Egocentric to Cooperative Play in Young Children: A Normative Study*.

Yeager, R. (2000) "A little boost of encouragement goes a long, long way" *Houston Area Association for the Education of Young Children Advocate* 19 (3).

index

about i am your child

I Am Your Child is a national, non-profit, non-partisan foundation dedicated to promoting public awareness about—and stronger societal investments in—early childhood development and school readiness. Founded in 1997 by Rob Reiner, I Am Your Child provides a wide variety of resources to parents, caregivers, parent educators and home visitors, child advocates, policymakers, and the media.

For **parents and caregivers**, the foundation has produced videos (with accompanying print materials) on such topics as school readiness, prenatal care, and setting limits. They are research-based, but very accessible. Available in English and Spanish, the videos are hosted by such personalities as LeVar Burton, Jamie Lee Curtis, Andy Garcia, Gloria Estefan, Whoopi Goldberg, Julia Louis-Dreyfus, Edward James Olmos, Phylicia Rashad, Cristina Saralegui and Maria Shriver. They also feature well-known child development experts, such as Dr. T. Berry Brazelton.

For **parent educators and child care providers**, I Am Your Child provides guidance on helping parents get the most out of its video and print materials.

For **child advocates, policy-makers, and the media**, the foundation offers insight, grounded in research, into key child development issues and strategies for improving young children's healthy development and school readiness.

I Am Your Child has received major support from the Bill and Melinda Gates Foundation, David and Lucile Packard Foundation, the California Endowment, Carnegie Corporation of New York, Johnson & Johnson, and IBM.

You can visit the foundation's website at www.iamyourchild.org.

about the authors

Janet Pozmantier, M.S., L.P.C., L.M.F.T., R.P.T., developed and currently administers the award-winning parent education program *Parents Under Construction*. She is a licensed professional counselor, marriage and family therapist, and registered play therapist, with a Master of Science degree in child development.

Joanne Go, M.S., E.I.S., B.A.T., is Community Education Director at ChildBuilders in Houston, Texas. She has a Master of Science degree in child development, is certified as an early intervention specialist, and has a Bachelor of Arts degree in teaching.

Laurie Segal Robinson, M.A., L.P.C., L.M.F.T., currently works as a parent education consultant to child care centers, assisting them with parent education concerns. She has a Master of Arts degree in clinical psychology, and is a licensed professional counselor and marriage and family therapist.

acknowledgements

AUTHORS' ACKNOWLEDGEMENTS
The authors thank LaVonne Carlson, Jennifer Williams, and Nancy Burke for their editorial wisdom and guidance. Each writer also thanks the families of the other writers for their patience and support. For their collective inspiration, wisdom, guidance, enthusiasm, and support . . . Joanne Go thanks the children and parents she has worked with through the years, Nancy Bewley, her writers' group, and her family; Janet Pozmantier acknowledges her parents, her husband and children, and her cowriters; and Laurie Segal Robinson thanks her husband and children.

PUBLISHERS ACKNOWLEDGEMENTS
DK Publishing would like to thank Raj Mankad for invaluable editorial assistance. **Models** Mary Atkinson, Markus, Robin and Sydnie Cano, Elizabeth and Grace Fithian, Dominique, Anthony and Erica Speciale, Sandra and Cailin Stollar, Lela and Liliana Su, Simon, Tracey, Luke and Shane Tasker, Jeff and Christopher Kai Toone, Jim and Evan Williamson, and John, Carline and Chloe Yup **Stylist** Daria Maneche **Make-up Artist** Isaac Olaizola **Additional photography credits** p 15 Rick Gomez/Corbis Stock Market; p 45 Jim Erickson/Corbis Stock Market; p 48 David Woods/Corbis Stock Market; p 51 LWA/Corbis Stock Market; p 46 Simon Brown; p 49 Jules Selmes; p 59 bottom left Roland Kemp; p 59 bottom right Michael Langford; p 87 Laura Dwight/Corbis.